On Film Editing

On Film Editing

An Introduction to the Art of Film Construction

EDWARD DMYTRYK

FOCAL PRESS
Boston • London

Focal Press is an imprint of Butterworth–Heinemann

Library of Congress Cataloging in Publication Data

Dmytryk, Edward.
  On film editing.
  1. Moving-pictures—Editing. I. Title.
TR899.D6 1984   778.5'35   84–4258
ISBN 0–240–51738–5

Butterworth–Heinemann
313 Washington Street
Newton, MA 02158–1626

20 19 18 17 16 15

Printed in the United States of America

Contents

Preface vii
Introduction ix

1. Titles and Definitions 1
2. Who Cuts the Film? 7
3. Smooth Cutting—The Ideal 11
4. The Cutter Begins 17
5. You've Got to Have a Reason 23
6. The Action Cut—and What Makes
   It Work 27
7. Keep It Fresh and Fast with the Overlap 35
8. Trying a Little Harder 43
9. Cutting Dialogue 47
10. The Reaction Is What Really Counts 65
11. If You Can't Make It Smooth,
    Make It Right 71
12. Knowing Your Audience 77
13. Dissolves: Why, How, and If 83
14. Editing—Simple and Pure 89
15. More of the Same 103
16. Rescuing the Actor 131
17. Where It All Began—The Montage 135

Epilogue 145
Filmography of Edward Dmytryk 147

Preface

It was the early 1930s. A very important guest, Baron Rothschild, was being given Paramount's version of the Grand Tour. One of his stops was my cutting room, where I was asked to say a few words by way of defining my craft.

I was young and enthusiastic. Some twenty minutes later, as I paused for breath, the Baron smiled.

"It would appear," he said, "that film editing *is* the art of filmmaking."

I agreed, trying to ignore the twinkle in his eyes. Of course, I was then a film editor. A few years later, when I became a director, I would have probably changed my pitch—but not too much.

Introduction

Today few people will deny that "The Film," as it is commonly called, is the most dynamic of all the arts, and none can argue with the statistics which show it to be, by long odds, the most popular art form in the world. However, many who try to analyze its power and appeal are brought up short by the collective nature of its creation. They can study, criticize, and debate the "art," but they find it very difficult to define the "artist."

One accepted judgment of today is that the film is created solely by the director—the "auteur"—and in a few instances—a very few—this may be true. Putting aside for a moment the claims of screenwriters, cinematographers, actors, and a number of other workers to at least some portion of the creative credit, there is one other craftsman without whom a film could hardly come into being—an artist who has it in his power to mold, improve, and even recreate a motion picture. That artist is the film editor.

"Once more I repeat," said Pudovkin, "that editing is the creative force of filmic reality." Ernest Lindgren agreed. "The development of film technique," he said, "has been primarily the development of editing."

These statements are as true today as they were 55 and 35 years ago. Not too long after Edwin S. Porter started experimenting with the intercutting of related and simultaneous action and D. W. Griffith decided to shoot a "close-up" to increase the dramatic impact of a player's reaction, filmmakers found that by means of a "cut" they could manipulate space, time, emotions, and emotional intensity to an extent limited only by their individual instincts and creative abilities. Film editing thus became the essence of "motion pictures." Without it, the best movie would be only a photographed stage play, and "the art of the cinema" would have remained an unarticulated phrase.

Editing brought film to life by bringing life to film. It was the chief ingredient in the creation of a new and more dynamic art form. After Griffith, the art of editing reached great heights in the hands of a few Russian filmmakers. Then it was severely depressed by the advent of sound, with its "fixative" tendencies. Finally, it escaped and entered a new and promising period in the 1940s, its liberation brought about largely by Orson Welles and his *Citizen Kane*. Now it is once again suffering through a period of banality, which is the inevitable result of the peculiar economic and so-called artistic demands of corporate television. To put it bluntly, the art of editing has all but expired as a vital development, and if Lindgren's thesis is correct, the development of film technique, as a whole, has all but expired with it.

So . . . this small book is written in the hope of helping the beginning director as well as the embryonic film editor. It is just possible that a reawakening of interest on the part of filmmakers in the still unexplored potential of film editing may bring about the long overdue renaissance of the filmmakers' art. For such an interest to arise, it is necessary that the primary filmmaker, the director, understand the importance of editing and that he learn how to incorporate it fully into his filmmaking technique. Certainly no director can claim to be an "auteur" unless he can edit or fully supervise the editing of his own films, and the extent to which a director's films approach the full potential of excellence will depend as much on his mastery of the editing craft as on his knowledge and practice of story and filming techniques.

On Film Editing

1

Titles and Definitions

There are as many levels in the practice of this craft as there are practicing craftsmen. They range from the "mechanical" to the truly creative, and when modified by the skill and ingenuity which any particular cutter may possess, as well as the input of directors and producers, they present us with the possibility of a nearly infinite number of styles and techniques and an almost equal number of results.

The use of the word *cutter* in the previous sentence was intentional. In the 1920s and early 1930s, a cutter who called himself a film editor would have been considered a snob. Then came the Wagner Labor Relations Act and unionization. In an attempt to raise the status of the craft, which was considered by the less knowledgeable executives of Hollywood to be five or six rungs from the top of the filmmaker's ladder, it was decided that *film editor* had a more imposing sound than *film cutter*, and henceforth that became the official terminology.*

*For the same reason, a cameraman became a *director of photography*; script clerks became *script supervisors*, even though absolutely no script supervision was involved in their work; a set designer became an *art director*; and so on, to a ridiculous degree. Eventually, the Screen Directors Guild was forced to demand, in contract bargaining, that no further craftsmen be gratuitously awarded the title of director of anything.

However, most film editors, at least in each other's company, still use the down-to-earth term *cutter* to define themselves and their profession.

It is probably safe to say that no two cutters will cut a film, or even a moderately lengthy sequence, in exactly the same way. So let us consider some of the varieties of workers in the field. First, let us look at one of that number who populate the fat part of the bell-shaped curve, the *mechanic*. Working as an apprentice, he (or she)* learns a few simple rules, follows the script and/or the director's instructions, and delivers a film to which the cutting has added not one whit of anything ingenious or original. On the contrary, his lackluster efforts may diminish the film's potential impact considerably. It is the mechanic's good fortune that so few directors, producers, and studio executives have the expertise with which to judge his contribution, although I have rarely encountered a member of any of these categories who did not consider himself to be one of the world's great film editors.

At the top of the scale is the *creative editor*, the person with an understanding of dramatic structure, a keen sense of timing, a compulsion to seek out the scene's hidden values—values which even the writer and the director may not have clearly grasped (believe me, it does happen!)—and a mastery of the technical skills needed to bring all these talents to bear on the film he edits. Unfortunately, there are very few creative cutters in the field, at least among those who edit other people's work. The reasons are clear, and a little sad.

On the average film, a cutter's status is usually beneath that of the director, the writer, the top actors, the producer, the photographer, the composer, and sometimes the set designer. And his salary is proportionate to his status. This state of affairs often induces a potentially brilliant cutter to seek a

---

*In the silent days, a large proportion of cutters were women. At Famous Players Lasky, where I worked, *all* the cutters were women. The advent of sound, with its complexities, led a number of executives to conclude that women could not handle sound-related technical problems, and many of them were discharged, never to return. However, the best of them survived, and within a few years, younger women joined them at the benches. For most of the life of motion pictures, a singularly male-oriented business, cutting has been the only craft that has fully utilized the talents of a fair percentage of women.

career offering greater rewards, even though his talents may not lie along other lines. Add to this the extremely long apprenticeship which assistant cutters are forced to serve, no matter how great their talents, and it is clear why so many quick, bright, and ambitious young men and women often opt for alternative careers. I have known several promising young men who have abandoned the cutting rooms because they were unwilling to spend 7 or 8 years at menial labor before getting permission to put scissors to film.

At the top of the scale lies another trap. Really fine, creative cutters quickly earn a "miracle man" reputation. Promotion, difficult to resist because of the increases in salary and status, inevitably follows, usually to the rank of director or, less frequently, producer. But these crafts demand their own special talents, and success is by no means assured. Indeed, the result is often tragic. A backward step is difficult to take, for obvious reasons, and many cutters, in classic adherence to the "Peter principle," persist in hanging on as second- or third-rate directors or producers rather than return to a highly respected cutter's bench. Only a handful of exceptional men and women have been content to spend their working lives exercising their rare talents in the relative obscurity of the cutter's cubicle.

To appreciate the role of editing in the filmmaking process, one must have some understanding of how a film is made. Working backward from the completed work, we find that the film is divided into a number of *sequences*, each sequence corresponding, let us say, to a chapter in a book or a scene in a play. Broadly speaking, a sequence has its own beginning, middle, and end, although these are not as clearly marked as they are in the film as a whole.

Each sequence, in turn, is divided into *scenes*, the number of such scenes varying from one to many. Example, in *Raiders of the Lost Ark*, the chase through the marketplace in the Arab town is one *sequence*, from the start of the chase to its conclusion with the hero's final escape. The *scenes* are those parts of the sequence which take place in any one location, whether they are as simple as one setup shot taking the actors through a narrow alley or as complex as the hero's confrontation with the assassin in black, a scene of considerable length that required a large number of setups.

The *scenes* consist of a number of *cuts*, or separate, individual pieces of film. Just as the sequence may consist of one or more scenes, so a scene may consist of one cut from a single setup or, more often, several cuts derived from two or more setups. There is no one-to-one correspondence between setups and cuts, since each setup may furnish a number of cuts, as usually occurs in the intercutting of matching close-ups in dialogue scenes.

The truth, then, is that in spite of the time, talent, and effort spent in writing, preparing, and shooting a film, it has no shape or substance until the hundreds, even thousands, of bits and pieces which go to make it are assembled. And it is here that the editor puts *his* stamp on the film. Every artist, if he *is* an artist, puts his own imprint on anything he does. Gilbert Stuart's portrait of Washington is not the same as Charles Peale's. Cortes, Picasso, and Kandinsky would each have painted the same Paris street in his own individual, widely different style. Three directors would make quite different films from the same script. All this is quite commonly accepted. But what is not so commonly known is that, given a free hand, three different cutters will create three different versions out of the same material, and the results of their labors will depend not only on the quality of the filmed scenes, but to a considerable degree, on the talents and skills of the editors themselves.

Needless to say, these skills come in different sizes, as do their effects on film. The glib phrase "saved in the cutting room" is heard not too infrequently in film circles. It sounds clever, but it hardly conforms to the facts. At the least, it is an exaggeration. The editor may improve a film by eliminating excessive and/or redundant dialogue, by selective editing of inadequate acting, by creative manipulation of the film's pace and the timing of reactions, by mitigating the weaknesses of badly directed scenes, and on rare occasions, by more unusual editorial maneuvers. Any or all of this activity presupposes a clever editor working on a more or less incompetently directed film. However, as often as not, a more or less incompetent editor is working on a cleverly directed film and not doing it justice. In any case, the editor works only with the material handed him by the director. Even if the editor creates a "miracle," the fact remains that that material carries *all* the ingredients of that miracle except, of course, for the creative ability brought to the cutting process by the editor. Finally, it must be borne in mind that although the editing "magic" is created in the cutting room, its creator is quite often *not* the cutter.

2

Who Cuts the Film?

Who, exactly, does edit the film. Usually, no single person, exactly. Although there have been a few notable exceptions, a good director always has the leading influence on the editing of his film, the value of that influence being proportional to his instinct for and knowledge of editing. An experienced producer can also have marked editorial input at this stage of the production. And a cutter of established reputation and proven ability can have the greatest influence of all, if only because he sets the editorial "tone" by making the first complete assembly.

In 1953, Karel Reisz, in his excellent book, *The Technique of Film Editing*, wrote, "In Hollywood . . . writers normally prepare their scripts in much greater detail and leave the director with the comparatively minor role of following the written instructions." If Hollywood writers, then or now, prepare their scripts in much greater detail, it is to aid the production staff in scheduling the film, not for shooting or editorial purposes. Quite to the contrary, no Hollywood director worth his salt would tailor his setups or his editing concepts to the script's measure. In more than 50 years as a cutter and director I have not known a single nonhyphenated writer with more

7

than an amateur's knowledge of cutting, and few Hollywood writers make any claim to editorial expertise. Most write master scenes and make no effort to indicate other than routine scene subdivisions. So the script writer, unless he also happens to be the director or producer of the film, can be eliminated as a contributor to its editing. And most writer-directors depend more on their cutters for editorial advice than they do on the "instructions" in their scripts, even if the scripts happen to be their own.

Editorial responsibility, then, narrows down to the director, the producer, and the film editor (with an occasional stray suggestion from a studio executive). Which one of these carries the main burden on any particular picture depends mostly on the director involved. It works something like this:

Most directors have had no "hands on" cutting experience. Members of this group exhibit a broad spectrum of behavior. A few may take little or no interest in the cutting. The wise ones will "glom onto" a good editor, when and if they find one; then they will adopt a supervisorial stance, making known their dramatic desires while leaving the execution of those desires in the editor's hands. Only a few will attempt precise cutting instructions.

For the conscientious cutter, these last are often a source of great trouble. Not knowing the patois of the cutting room,* they are usually unable to verbalize their concepts with accuracy. Their "specific" cutting instructions almost always amount to editorial double-talk, which the cutter must then translate into workable and effective ideas. So the question becomes: Should the cutter make the cuts exactly as the director spelled them out, or should he cut the film *his* way to arrive at the results which *he thinks* the director wanted, bas-

---

*Every craft has its own language, or terminology, most of which is unintelligible to the layman. The special idioms of the sciences are generally acknowledged, but the language of even those professions which deal with the general population, such as teaching or politics, and as such should be completely understandable is often arcane or esoteric. (See?) Many of the film terms as used in schools of the cinema, especially those dealing with genre or theory, have never been heard on a studio lot, a condition that will probably change as more film school graduates take their places in the "real" film world. But even then, since the cutting room is far removed from the sound stage, few crew members will understand the cutters' special jargon.

ing his judgment on his interpretation of the director's expressed instructions?

The wise cutter will, of course, follow the second procedure, making the cuts in question *his* way to arrive at the desired result. And, if he is a very good cutter, that result will be, in the director's words, "exactly what I was looking for."

The less secure or more restricted cutter will try to follow the director's precise instructions and usually will find himself with a mess on his hands. Let me cite an experience of my own as an example.

On one of my first editorial assignments, I presented a first cut which was perhaps 20 minutes longer than optimum length. The running time was by no means unusually excessive and called for a routine trimming to bring it down to size. Over a period of 2 or 3 days the producer and the director reviewed the film, running and rerunning a sequence at a time. Instead of eliminating whole scenes, or even sequences, as is customary (and generally desirable), they called for the elimination of a phrase here, a modifying clause there, even, occasionally, a single word, necessitating what is called a "hemstitching job." So many cuts of this kind were demanded that a smooth, understandable cut was impossible, but the supervising editor advised me to make the cuts exactly as asked for, even though he too, considered them incompetent.

The cuts were made, the director and producer viewed the recut version in silence, then marched down to the executive offices to demand my removal from the film and dismissal from the studio. My career hung by a thread. Fortunately, the supervising editor, Roy Stone (may his courage be ever remembered), gave his version of the episode. I was permitted to recut the film properly, and all turned out well.

I was 22 years old, and I had learned one of the most important lessons of my life: In any creative effort, one must do one's own thing, even if that thing is being done in response to another's order. To do otherwise is to seriously risk a result which will please neither the requestor nor the executor.

On the great majority of films, then, all the actual "hands on" cutting is done by the film editor, with the director and/or the producer supplying most, if not all, of the creative

ideas involving changes in continuity, in the editing or elimination of scenes or sequences, and in the manipulation of acting emphasis and audience attention. The part the cutter plays
in these proceedings depends on the director's faith in the cutter's talent and on his willingness to allow the cutter to par-
ticipate in the creative process.

But, whatever the degree of that participation, the cutter
still has almost complete control over the tempo and pacing of
the film, and here he can do great damage or perform small
miracles. Since tempo and pace are largely the result of technical manipulation of cuts, a technique outside the average
director's sphere of expertise, lack of finesse in these areas,
though frequently quite apparent, often remains uncorrected,
and even an expert critic will rarely know where to place the
blame.

Naturally, those few directors with a great deal of practical
cutting experience are fully aware of this important aspect of
editing, and unless they are fortunate enough to have editors
who match or surpass them in editing intuition and technical
ability, they will insist on cutting their own films. Some will
allow the editor to make the "rough cut," to their instructions, while a few will undertake even that burdensome task.
But all will make the final cut with their own hands, fine-tun-
ing the film to their own satisfaction. This operation is as
important to a film as it is to a racing-car engine or a sym-
phony orchestra, and *only* the person actually handling the
film can properly make these desirable and necessary adjust-
ments.

3

Smooth Cutting—The Ideal

Film is a deceptive art—in many ways. Its collaborative nature is axiomatic, yet more than in most art forms, that collaboration is hidden from the audience. In a good film, the whole will always be greater than the sum of its parts. Every honest filmmaker strives to make a film which so enthralls the viewer that he lives and breathes only with the beings on the screen. If that viewer, during his first look at the film, is critically conscious of the sets, the photography, the acting, the director's "touches," the "brilliance" of the dialogue or the musical score, the good director knows he has come up short of perfection. A film's first viewing should evoke emotional, not critical, reaction. Nothing so warms the heart of the director of a dramatic film as an audience which sits quietly for minutes after the end title, digesting lingering thoughts and emotions, gathering itself for the return to reality.

This lack of eclectic awareness, or of technical appreciation, is especially true of editing. The finer the cutter's technique, the less noticeable is his contribution. And this oversight persists. No nonprofessional viewer will remember the cutting, even in postviewing analysis, since most cuts are specifically contrived to pass unnoticed. If the film is well shot and well cut, the viewer will perceive it as a motion picture which seems to flow in continuous, *unbroken* movement on a single strip of film. At times, even if a film is *not* well shot, an extremely clever cutter can still shape it into a smooth, continuous narrative.

So the good cutter finds satisfaction in the appreciation and applause of those of his peers, associates, and superiors who are aware of the travail and brain beating he undergoes to arrive at a result which few will notice. Humility is one of the cutter's strongest characteristics.

The conditions which make "smooth" cutting possible do not all arise spontaneously in the cutting room. The ideal of invisibility is achieved through a series of steps. The first, and one of the most important, can be taken only by the film's director.

Many directors have little understanding of the needs of the editor. Strange to say, some of our best directors have exhibited shortcomings in this area. Even stranger is the fact that such shortcomings have not noticeably diminished the quality of their films, at least not to the average viewer. On careful analysis, even a good many of our "classics" display tortuous transitions, improper "screen direction," and unimaginative composition. Does this prove that expertise in any or all of these areas is nonessential? By no means.

What it does prove, or at least indicate, is that there are many facets to any film, and all of them need not be first rate for that film to have audience appeal. A good film can be badly photographed on inferior stock (e.g., *Open City*) and still be a hit. A good film can survive a mediocre score or even sloppy editing if the indispensable major elements are present in strength. The only sure stiflers of appreciation and enjoyment are badly written stories, careless dramatic structuring, inadequately developed characters, and funereal pacing.

None of this is meant to imply that a director may lightly ignore the "minor" essentials. But if he does, someone will have to cover for him—and that someone is the film editor. Cosmetic applications, however, rarely equal competence at the source, and a film made by a director with limited cinematic knowledge will always fall short of its true potential, even though its faults may be cleverly concealed.

As the director plans his setups for a scene or sequence, he should anticipate where key cuts will be made, at least in cutting from one master setup to another. This means, for instance, that at the point of the cut there should be a marked difference in size, or angle, or number of characters (or all three) between the two setups. If the first setup shows, let us say, four players at full height, the next setup should *not* show the same four actors at the same full height from the same point of view. A close similarity in two contiguous cuts will guarantee a cut that "jumps," i.e., is noticeable to the viewer as a change of scene.*

It may seem illogical, but a decided change, e.g., cutting from the four shot to a close shot of one of the group, will make a smooth, unnoticeable transition, especially if the close shot shows a reaction or response to something said or done by another member of the group. However, the incoming cut should not present a point of view that will interrupt the flow of the scene, thus distracting the viewer and losing his attention.

Perhaps the greatest sinner of all is the "clever" director who "cuts in the camera." The phrase, which can be used in several contexts, usually signifies that the director, in any particular "take," shoots only that portion of the scene which he expects to use as one complete cut, whether it be an action in a full shot or a reaction or single line of dialogue in a close-up. This technique is used in the false belief that it saves film, time, and money, or because the director fears the cutter will

---

*In film parlance, the word *cut* has several meanings, all easily understood in context. As a verb, *to cut*, it signifies the act of cutting together a number of scenes into a finished film, or "work print." Beyond that, the word *cut* serves as a noun in several contexts: first, an unbroken strip of film recording all or part of a single setup; second, the splice, or joint, between two cuts of the first kind; third, some or all of the sequences which have been deleted from the film during the editing process, and fourth, the word is used to describe the total work print, especially when denoting the number of times the film has been reworked, as in *rough cut, first cut, director's cut, final cut,* and so forth.

play fast and loose with the material if given too many options. The technique is self-defeating for two reasons:

1.   It depends on sticking to strict "story-boarding" or cutting to script, thus "setting" the film prematurely and obviating any opportunity for later improvement or enhancement.
2.   It is clearly bad directional technique, since it affords the actors little or no opportunity to "get into the scene" and results in superficial, often stiff, performances.

A close relative of the director who "cuts in the camera" is the director who ignores cutting and shoots long master shots, "theater style," with little or no coverage. Although this kind of shot can be advantageous on rare occasions, most extended scenes need proper coverage for dramatic emphasis or constructive deletion.

Ernst Lubitsch, certainly one of the great directors in Hollywood history, once made this fatal mistake. He shot a dramatic scene in a single master shot, allowing for no cutaways, considering it completely satisfactory as it played. The preview audience failed to see it his way. Severe pruning was called for, but no protection setups had been shot. The entire scene had to be refilmed in a number of setups at considerable labor and expense.

Even if the director feels that a particular scene plays at its best in a single setup—and almost every director has resorted to this technique at one time or another—basic wisdom demands that he protect himself against the occasional misjudgment. Such *protection* (the actual term used in this context) is cheap insurance and is obtained by a simple procedure, one known and used for more than half a century. In cutting room jargon it is known as "cutting to the kitchen stove." Translated, it means that a shot of one of the players involved in the scene, an observer outside it, or even some inanimate object on the set (or location) can be used as a cutaway from the master scene if it is later decided that a deletion in the scene is desirable. Such a shot, made on the spot, will take relatively little time and will disturb the schedule and the budget far less than if it has to be made at some future date.

The truth is that every good director who has risen from the cutting ranks and who feels secure in his cutting concepts still "protects" himself liberally. He knows better than anyone how often additional cinematic values can be supplied through the cutting process.

4

The Cutter Begins

At a purely technical level, each editor develops his own approach to his work, although that approach will most likely be a variation of one of those few which time and trial have proven to be the most efficient. Here, I will concentrate on the method which works best for me and which, naturally, is the one I can support wholeheartedly. However, the beginning cutter can modify this procedure to suit his own needs and, what is more important, his special talents.

Quite possibly, the cutter's first chores will be in the area of preproduction. This usually means a search for needed "stock" material. For instance, before starting production on *The Caine Mutiny*, I visited the Naval Archives in Washington, D.C., and reviewed many thousands of feet of film which had been shot by a host of photographers during naval preparation and action in the Pacific during World War II.

I had hoped to find usable footage of the great typhoon which scattered our huge invasion fleet in the latter days of World War II, but I had been naive. Cameramen can hardly be expected to stand on a heaving ship deck during the height of such a storm, and the speed of color film in the early 1940s was wholly inadequate for filming under the prevailing light conditions. Eventually, of course, the whole of the typhoon sequence had to be shot in production. However, a number of shots of battleships firing practice salvos and bombarding island installations in preparation for marine landings were selected for use in the film.

"Stock shots" are used in many films, especially those involving sports, such as football games, automobile or horse racing, and so forth. On occasion, selection of such material may be delayed until postproduction editing, but it is better done before the start of shooting so that film shot in production can more accurately match the stock selected.

The cutter's work on the film itself starts on the day the first "rushes" are viewed. The takes of the previous day's shooting are customarily assembled in the lab or by the assistant cutter, most often in the order in which they were shot. At the company running, the editor (and usually his assistant) sits at the director's side—for two reasons: First, the cutter lists the director's take selections, where more than one take of a scene has been printed. Second, he makes notes of the particular takes, or portions of takes, which the director selects for use in the first cut. Some directors offer little advice at this stage, trusting the editor to make the best use of the filmed material; others give precise, detailed instructions for the use of the specific takes, angles, or portions thereof (see Chapter 9, Figure 4).

One day's shooting on even a moderately liberal schedule will hardly supply enough material for actual cutting. It may take the director two, three, or more days to complete a scripted scene or sequence. As the film is released to the cutter, his assistant will usually reassemble the takes "in sequence," i.e., in script order, with the close shots and close-ups placed immediately after the master shots covering the same material. An exact assembly is rarely possible, since portions of a single take may be used as cuts at different places in the finished sequence. But the more closely the reassembly can approach the eventual rough-cut alignment, the easier it will be for the editor to organize his cutting routine.

Now, an item of great importance: When the assembly is ready, it should be viewed on the big screen. One viewing may be sufficient, but more often, especially if the demands of the sequence, technically or dramatically, are appraised as severe, the material should be reviewed time and again until the cutter is quite sure which portions of which takes he wants to use and where he anticipates making his cuts.

Many editors shape their editing concepts on the Moviola, a technique I consider decidedly inferior. One does not see the same things on a small Moviola screen, or even on the somewhat larger, though fuzzier, flatbed screen, that one sees in a theater. The audience sees its films only on the "big screen," and since every cut should be made with the audience in mind, the cutter must try to see each bit of film as the viewer in the theater will eventually see it. (Even a moderate-sized television screen offers far more scope than a Moviola; therefore, it too presents a somewhat different "picture" for the viewer's inspection.)

The usual theatrical films, excluding art films, *film verite*, and so forth, are meant to appeal to the largest possible audience, and sound theories of filmmaking, including cutting, are based on this fact. Staging, setups, and cutting should always be conceived to show the viewer what he should see at every point in the film. Sometimes it is what the viewer, whether or not he is aware of it, *wants* to see; sometimes it is what the viewer, whether or not he likes it at the moment, *should* see; and sometimes (quite often, really) it is what the director and/or cutter manipulate him into *thinking* he wants to see. But a cut, or even a short portion of a cut, which the viewer cares nothing about is a waste of time. All this may seem obvious, yet the verges of the road to success are strewn with the bodies of filmmakers who ignored this principle and brought in films which, wholly or in part, audiences found flat and unentertaining.

This is why the cutter should make his choices on the big screen. "Holding" a cut because of the beauty of a composition or the clever "bit" of a secondary character is of no value if the cut under consideration had delivered its full message. Lingering on a scene for some subjectively esoteric reason is one of the pitfalls of editing. The viewer, engrossed in the film, may not be seeing the cutter's "vision" at all. In cutting as in directing, objectivity is of the utmost importance—self-indulgence leads only to disaster.

When the cutter feels he has his cutting concept well in mind, the next step is to the cutter's bench. Here, too, routines differ. In preparation for the actual cutting, some editors like to have the assembled rushes broken down into individual takes. These are arranged on the bench in sequence order and then selected by the cutter as he proceeds to stitch the scenes together.

Others prefer to cut directly off the assembled reels, pulling the takes down into a film bin as they select their cuts. Although some takes may have to be pulled out and set aside for later use, I find this method produces the least disorder. But, whichever technique is used, pieces of film will always be scattered helter-skelter—in the bin, on film hooks, and around the cutter's neck. Here is where a good assistant is invaluable. Keeping "trims" (i.e., unused portions of takes) instantly locatable is a requisite for smooth operation and efficient use of time, because the "trim" of the first rough assembly may be the inspired cut in a later version.

Two distinct machines, or pieces of equipment, are used in the cutting procedure. The first, the *Moviola*, dates from the early days of film; it is preferred by most Hollywood editors. The second, called the *flatbed*, used by European editors, is of comparatively recent origin.

Having worked with both, my preference is decidedly for the Moviola. Frequent removal and replacement of film and sound tape are essential to the style of cutting discussed in this book; it is more easily and quickly accomplished on the Hollywood machine. Except for the beginnings and ends of most sequences, a cut should rarely be made "straight across;" that is, the picture and tape should *not* be cut at their matching points. No matter how small, the overlapping of cuts requires careful manipulation if synchronization is to be maintained. Cutters who use the flatbed are more inclined to cut straight across, which leads to a "stop and start" technique and sloppiness. In addition, a film should be cut primarily for the picture, since that is what is seen on the screen, and this kind of film handling is more accurately accomplished on the Moviola.

However, in the final stages of editing, especially when *a* and *b* tracks are used for sound overlaps, as well as for sound and music editing, the flatbed is unbeatable. Every cutting facility should have one or more at hand.

Now, an important step: When the sequence is finally assembled, it should be laid aside. Cutters who are not quite sure of themselves choose to review their efforts immediately. They risk a very frustrating experience. Since all the cuts made are fresh in mind, the cutter is sure to anticipate each one rather than go with the flow of the sequence. Consequently, each cut is almost sure to "jump," and the cutter will be inclined to assume the jumps are caused by inadequate matching rather than by his anticipation. He will then attempt immediate corrections. The result can be pretty messy.

If the newly cut sequence is put aside for a number of days— even weeks—while another sequence or two is cut in the interim, the original cuts will have been forgotten and will pass on the screen without anticipation. All properly made cuts should now be unnoticeable. Only if the cuts jump at this stage will there be need for technical correction. As for the more demanding *editorial* correction, this is a whole different story which will be addressed in its proper turn. For immediate consideration, we will take up the problems of cutting technique.

5

You've Got to Have a Reason

The first two basic rules of cutting are as follows:

Rule 1. *Never* make a cut without a positive reason.

Rule 2. When undecided about the exact frame to cut on, cut *long* rather than short.*

Cuts should be conceived on the big screen, but they can be made only on the Moviola. To put it more simply, based on his viewing of the assembled material, the cutter decides where he wants to change angles, where to move into a close shot or cut back to a long shot, and where to cut to a reaction or a response. But on the big screen the film flashes by at 24 frames a second, a cut takes only 1 frame, and a cutter can

---

*The rules of cutting, as stated, are mine. Some of those which I will lay down in this book have been observed for many years, a few before my time, but they have never, to my knowledge, been codified. Experienced editors will probably agree with most of my rules. However, if you want to question one now and then—have fun.

hardly spot the exact frame to cut on in this infinitesimal space of time.* Therefore, the cutter must view his film on the Moviola, where he can start, stop, run forward, or run backward as quickly, as slowly, and as often as he wishes. He must be able to stop on the proverbial dime, and he often needs to. In short, it is on the Moviola that he finds the *exact* frame to leave one scene and the *exact* frame to enter the next.

The word *exact* is stressed because I believe that the proper cut can be made only at a single point. Obviously, cutting three or four frames to either side of the hypothetically ''perfect'' cut will make a difference of only 3/24ths or 4/24ths of a second—hardly enough to bother a viewer who consumes 5/24ths of a second to, literally, blink an eye. But why be 1/8th of a second off target if you can be perfect? Beyond this purely ethical consideration, when making an ''action cut,'' three frames too much or too little on one side or the other can effectively spoil the match.

Now, to expand on rule 1: This rule may seem obvious, but the key here is ''*positive* reason.'' I have known cutters who felt that if they allowed a scene to run more than a certain arbitrary number of feet without a cut, they were not doing their job. But a cut should never be made only because the cutter feels the prevailing cut is too long. ''Too long'' is a very elastic measurement. A cut can be too long at 1 foot and not long enough at 500 feet.

In *Broken Lance*, I shot two scenes that ran about 10 minutes, or 900 feet, each. (One-thousand feet is as much film as the average 35 mm magazine will hold.) One scene was played by Spencer Tracy and Richard Widmark, the other by Tracy and E.G. Marshall. These three were great actors who could ''hold'' an audience as well as anyone in films. Also, in both instances, I used a moving camera and moving actors; i.e., the camera could move from a long shot into a close shot and back again as the scene progressed, and the actors could move from a full shot into a close-up when greater intensity was needed.

---

*Technically speaking, a cut or splice is made on the ''frame line'' between two frames of picture. It occupies the space between two sprocket holes, or one-quarter of a frame. In addition, since its movement across the projection aperture is blocked from view by a synchronized projection machine shutter, it is never seen at all. What is seen is the change from one scene to the next.

In the finished film, both scenes played at full length without a cut. The scenes were so tight and so dramatic that intercutting would not have helped in the least. I had, of course, made a "protection" take for each scene (see Chapter 3), but neither one was needed.

I have also, in certain action or montage sequences, used cuts as short as six frames, or one-quarter of a second. It took just that long, and no longer, for the cuts to deliver their total messages.

As a sequence is being cut, the cutter should know where a particular setup most effectively presents the information needed for that particular part of the scene. In other words, he will stay with a shot as long as that shot is the one which best delivers the required information and cut to another shot only when the new cut will better serve the purposes of the scene, whether because the size is more effective, the composition is more suitable, or the interpretation is superior.

One cuts to a close-up, for instance, to enhance a response or intensify a reaction. Deep feeling—emotion—is usually best expressed through the eyes, and the closer the shot, the more clearly the emotion can be seen and felt by the viewer. However, cutting to a close-up when *no* enhancement of emotion is called for is not only wasteful, but tends to diminish the value of subsequent close-ups when they are legitimately needed. The overuse of *any* effect diminishes its true worth.

There are other, though infrequent occasions, when similar emotional intensity will play better in longer shots. In *Mirage*, Gregory Peck enters Walter Mathau's office and finds him strangled to death. After a brief moment of shocked inaction, Peck vents his grief and rage through violence, smashing furniture and throwing a chair through a window. Obviously, this scene played best in a series of wide shots, where the full range of Peck's righteous anger could be given full play.

In short, as long as the scene is playing at its best in the selected angle, leave it alone! The only reason for using another cut is to improve the scene.

Rule 2 may also seem obvious, yet how often have I seen it violated! Every cut is the result of a conscious decision, hard or easy, and as any psychologist can testify, making a decision can be a traumatic experience. The more options available, the more difficult are the decisions. I have often seen an inexperienced cutter agonize for hours over a single cut and regret it instantly when the cut was finally made, feeling sure that one of his other options was preferable.

The rule that applies in school examinations also applies, logically enough, in cutting: The first immediate and instinctive choice is more likely than not to be the right one. Experience will eventually teach a cutter exactly where to make his cut the first time around, and the decision will scarcely make a blip on his mind, but if there is any doubt as to how many frames should precede or follow a reaction, let us say, it is wiser to leave the cut a little long. Trimming a cut down to proper size at a later run-through will prove to be simple—and much, much more neat. Splicing a few frames back onto a scene which has been lopped short makes "jumpy" viewing, and a cut full of such amendments makes proper visualization difficult and perceptive judgment impossible.

6

The Action Cut— and What Makes It Work

Rule 3: Whenever possible, cut "in movement."

The "action cut" is the first bit of cutting lore learned by every apprentice. Excluding cuts made at the beginnings and ends of sequences and self-contained scenes, cuts to reactions or responses, and cuts involving exchanges of dialogue, the cutter should look for some movement of the actor who holds the viewer's attention and use that movement to trigger the cut from one scene to the next. A broad action will offer the easier cut, but even a slight movement of some part of the player's body can serve to initiate a cut which will be "smooth" or invisible.

As an example, let us take a very common sequence of cuts: In a full shot, a player enters an office, approaches a desk, and sits down in the desk chair. The full shot has established the scene's setting, and it is now necessary to zero in on the character as he proceeds about his business, so a close shot of him at the desk is in order.

The best place to cut to the close shot is as the actor sits, and here we have three options: (1) We can leave the full shot early, as the actor reaches his chair, and show the complete action of sitting in a close shot which centers on the chair. (2) We can allow the actor to sit in the full shot, cutting to the close shot only after that action is completed. (3) We can cut somewhere between the cutting points of the first two options. For most good editors, the last would be the automatic choice.

The exact cutting point would depend on the cutter's sense of proper timing. All exceptional editors have this sense to an exceptional degree. In our hypothetical example, the cut would probably be made at just about the point where the seat of the chair and that of the player are about to collide. (Even though that point is hidden by the desk, it can be deduced from the movement of the body, a type of deduction often required in cutting ([see p. 33]).

Cutting early would present us with some footage of the player's midsection, not exactly an inspiring image. The late cut would carry the long shot past the viewer's point of tolerance, however slightly. The cut at the midpoint avoids these two faults, as well as some others to be discussed later, while enabling us to take advantage of the magic of the "action cut." If there are problems with differences of position or variation in speed of movement (which sometimes occur as the result of sloppy staging), the timing of the cut might have to be modified, but the modification would be a forced compromise, not the cut of choice.

In the reverse action, also seen in virtually every film, the player rises from his chair in the close shot, and the fuller shot continues his movement.* Here the cut would probably come some 6 to 10 frames *after* the start of the action in the close shot. The longer shot would pick up the actor's movement at nearly the same spot. Exact matching of position, however, might not result in the smoothest cut, for reasons to be

---

*The experienced camera operator will maintain a fixed camera position, allowing the actor to rise out of the close shot. He will also set his composition at full height in the long shot. He knows the cut will probably be made during the rise and that a tilting camera movement at that point would spoil it.

explained shortly. Often an action overlap of 3 to 5 frames is desirable.

Contrary to common belief, the action cut does not require a measurable difference in image size. It is possible to cut from, let us say, a close-up of a player turning to his right, then have him complete his turn in another close-up, of similar size, shot from the new direction. It is even possible to move straight in, with no change in view line, from a close shot to a close-up, where the differences in size and range of movement are minimal. But this kind of cutting requires the most exquisite kind of timing, and relatively few cutters can execute it properly.

Often a cut must be made at a point where, unlike our previous examples, no broad movement is available. A player may already be seated, for instance, and the demands of the scene may call for a cut to a closer shot. In such a case, any movement—a turn of the head, for instance, or the raising of an arm as the player lifts a cup of coffee or a cigarette to his mouth—will, when precisely timed, serve to camouflage the cut. The important consideration here is that there be just enough movement to catch the viewer's attention.

Some cutters prefer to cut just before the start of a movement or immediately after its completion, but few, if any, of the top editors follow this practice. In situations of this kind, the "static" cut cannot be intelligently rationalized, and it is excusable only if the cutter is eliminating waste footage. Then he is merely making the best of an imperfect situation. If the timing of the action, as shot, is satisfactory, the action cut will always make the smoother transition.

However, most of the cuts in a modern film, with its emphasis on dialogue, cannot be made so conveniently. A player looks offscreen at something or someone, and a cut to that something or someone is in order. However, at the moment of looking, the player is usually quite still, as in the well-worn phrase, "His gaze was fixed upon. . . . " Obviously, no action cut is possible, yet a smooth cut can be made. But how? Or consider a dialogue scene in which two people are seated on a couch or at a table, riding in a car, or strolling down the lane talking to each other for minutes at a time, often without apparent movement, especially in their close-ups. Still, frequent cuts must be made to the speaker or to the listener's reaction. Here, too, smooth cutting is quite possible. But how?

By creating a "diversion" of sorts, which is also the principle at work in the action cut. But before we can discuss the principle, we must build a hypothesis,* and to do that, we will examine a close relative of the action cut, one that deals with entrances and exits.

An actor exits a scene by walking out of the *left* side of the screen, and we follow him as he enters the next scene *from the right.* This is proper "screen direction," and it is always shot this way (see Figures 1 and 2). Good editing practice rules that the cut away from the first scene should occur at the point where the actor's *eyes* exit the frame. The cut to the second scene should be made from 3 to 5 frames ahead of the point at which his eyes reenter the frame at the opposite side of the screen. (The cadence of his step also comes into play, but it has no bearing at this point.)

But why, when the actor appears in the second cut at the opposite side of the screen from his point of exit (which, on the wide screen, can be quite a separation), is such a cut, when properly made, completely acceptable to the viewer as a smooth, continuous action? Because his vision has been

Figure 1   Figure 2

---

*The building of this hypothesis took years of careful analysis and one moment of inspiration. Like the popular representations of the structure of the atom, it is purely a "construction" which may have no relation to the actual truth. However, it does what all good hypotheses should do—it works. Properly applied to any cut, or to the cutting concept as a whole, it will deliver a smooth, steadily flowing film.

"diverted" by the apparently awkward eye movement across the width of the screen.

At the point of the cut, two things happen. First, the actor's eyes or face, usually the viewer's center of interest, leave the screen. Second, as a result, the *viewer's* eyes, which have been following the actor's movement, encounter the darkness at the screen's edge. These two actions cause a reaction—the viewer's eyes swing back toward the center of the screen, then continue to its right edge, drawn there by the entrance of the actor in the new cut. All this has happened, quite unconsciously, in a fraction of a second, not nearly long enough for the viewer to be aware of the passage of time or to notice the cut which has slipped by in the interim. For—and this is the most important factor in the process—the viewer's eyes have been unfocused during their forced move, and he has seen nothing with clarity.

Experiments in reading long ago established that a reader's eyes cannot focus while moving, and short pauses to focus on words or small groups of words are an essential part of the reading process. The same holds true for someone looking at the screen. As his eyes move, sharp focus is impossible. Therefore, if the cut, lasting 1/24th of a second, can be made while the viewer consumes 1/5th of a second in moving his eyes, the cut will pass unnoticed. The trick is to get an audience of viewers to move their eyes en masse at the desired instant.

Hints have been around for some time. Some cutters have long been aware of one such "trick"; that is, cutting on a sharp sound—a door slam, for instance—to disguise a cut. Sharp noises cause the viewer to blink, which, as noted earlier, will take approximately 1/5th of a second. The blink is the equivalent of the eye movement in the exit-entrance cut or in the action cut. The "operator" in all these cuts is the distraction which causes movement or closure of the eyes. The cutter makes his cut as the viewer's eyes blink or are caught by the movement on the screen, much as a magician masks a move requiring camouflage by distracting the eyes of his audience with the broad sweep of his cape or a sharp movement of his "decoying" arm.

Filmmakers have often resorted to "deception" in order to

deliver the "truth." The 3 to 5 frame overlap mentioned in relation to the action cut is one example of such a deception. It is best analyzed in an examination of the exit-entrance cut. The overlapping (or repeated) 3 to 5 frames at the beginning of the second cut are redundant and are meant to be so. The viewer will, in a sense, miss them, since they flash by on the screen during the fraction of a second when his eyes are moving from left to right. When his eyes are refocused, the viewer sees the proper continuation of the actor's cross, not the short redundant overlap (see Figure 3).

If the cut were made to match exactly, what the viewer would miss during the eye movement would be frames essential to smooth action. The short hiatus would now register on the viewer's mind as a tiny jump forward in the action.

An overlap made to accommodate the viewer's "blind spot" is useful in most action cuts. But it is quite a subtle technique practiced by relatively few editors. Its absence from a film will

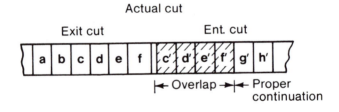

Figure 3

hardly destroy that film for the audience. In "static" cuts, however, the subject of the next chapter, the "blind spot" overlap is absolutely essential for good cutting, and no cutter should be ignorant of its proper use.

Oh, yes, the cadence of the step, which was by-passed on page 30. Most people have a strong sense of rhythm as expressed in marching, dancing, chanting, and other rhythmic activities. If this rhythm is needlessly disturbed, so is the viewer. Therefore, when cutting from one shot of a person walking to another in which the walking continues (as in an exit-entrance cut), care must be taken to make sure that the walker's foot hits the ground (or floor) in perfect cadence. If possible, the cut should be of the same foot, but failure to match feet is not nearly as disruptive as breaking the cadence of the walking. Cutting at the instant the foot hits the floor also helps to accomplish a smoother transition.

If the shots are too close to show the legs or feet, the proper cadence can be deduced from a careful examination of the movement of the actor's body. The rhythm of movement must be maintained even if the cut has to be shortened or lengthened by a few frames. In this case, sustaining proper rhythm is less disturbing than a slightly imperfect cut.

7

Keep It Fresh and Fast with the Overlap

Cutters, on the whole, are a conscientious lot, but inevitably some are ignorant, some are careless, and some are lazy. The first condition is lamentable, the second correctible, but the third is unforgivable. The lazy cutter cheats not only his director, his producer, and his employer, but he also cheats the viewer. A cutter who cuts "straight across" because overlapping takes more time and greater effort (which it certainly does) puts out a film which falls short of its potential.

Let us take a simple example—our old acquaintance, the exit-entrance cut. Quite a few working editors and almost all amateurs will allow the actor to make a full exit in the first cut and then hold the scene a number of frames more before cutting away. This kind of cutting is wrong on every count, whether technical or aesthetic, for the following reasons:

1.   It violates the rule concerning the viewer's eye movement.
2.   It extends a scene which no longer has any meaning or interest for the viewer.

35

3.   It increases the length of the film to no useful pur-
     pose.

(1) Has been discussed in depth in the preceding chapter, except for one aspect. If the viewer looks toward an incoming
cut and no cut appears, he will search the scene still on the
screen for what he assumes the filmmaker wants him to see.
(Unless he is deceived too often, the viewer will *always*
believe the filmmaker has some reason for everything he puts
on the screen.) When his search is rewarded with some footage
of an empty set, he will be confused or disappointed, neither
of which reactions recommends the cut.

(2) If the viewer is not confused or disappointed, he will
simply be bored. It has been many years since a mere picture
projected on the screen was considered amazing or amusing.
Every part of a film must deliver its message, but the only
message delivered by redundant frames of film is that the cutter was inept or too lazy to cut them off.

(3) This is an important consideration that is often a factor
in a film's appeal. A few extra frames may seem to give little
cause for concern, and if they appeared only once or twice in a
film, this might be true. But there are many cuts which lend
themselves to this special kind of carelessness, and when such
a fault is often repeated, the total amount of unprofitable film
can be considerable.

The most serious aspect of this miscut, however, is its
immediate effect on the viewer. A mental "hiccup" of this
sort interrupts the flow—hence the pacing—of the film, and
pacing is a key factor in raising the viewer's involvement up to
the highest possible level. Obviously, a series of such hiccups,
recurring throughout the film, can be harmful indeed.

Let us probe this concept a bit more deeply. Practical filmmakers have long held that the viewer should remain completely unaware of technique—all technique, whether that of
the actor, the cameraman, the writer, the director, or the cutter. In art, the obvious is a sin. Some aspects of this principle
have already been discussed. Now let us examine a special
case.

The setting is a desert road in New Mexico—John Ford
country. A stagecoach rumbles toward the viewer and passes
through and out of the scene. The cutter allows the shot to

linger on the "painted desert" as the dust slowly settles to earth. If the viewer murmurs to himself or to his companion, "What a beautiful shot," we have stayed with the cut too long. The viewer is appreciating our shot, not the film; he has become aware of our cinematic composition, our technique.

However, it *is* possible to let the viewer enjoy the beauty of the setting as part of the film as a whole. If we *start* the shot with the same beautiful landscape, the viewer will appreciate it at least as much, but will be accepting it in the context of the story. Most probably, of course, the stagecoach will already be seen in the distance. But even if it cannot be seen, even if, as yet, no action takes place on the screen, the viewer, while reacting to the scene's beauty, will also be anticipating some action pertaining to the film, looking for the stagecoach perhaps, thus again placing the scene into the context of the film. However, by the time the coach passes the camera, the viewer is ready for a change of scene.

Rule 4: The "fresh" is preferable to the "stale."

If, for some valid reason, a few *frames* must be tacked onto the end of one cut or the beginning of the next, or if, because of the need for exposition or background establishment, as in the preceding example, a few *feet* must be added to the end of one cut or the beginning of the next, always choose to place the extra footage at the beginning of the new, or incoming, cut. The reason is obvious, but often ignored.

In the case of the stagecoach scene, the reason for adding the extra footage to the beginning of the shot is easily understood. In the case of the few frames, however, the logic may not be so easily grasped. But the same rule is at work in both instances. Let us return to the exit-entrance cut for our example.

The first cut has played itself out on the screen, and for the duration of the cut, the set, or background, has been in full view. To linger on it after our actor has left the scene is to leave our viewer with "cold coffee." The second cut, however, is fresh to the eye and to the mind, and if it is necessary to add a number of frames before the actor enters the scene, the viewer has, at least, a new setting to examine and integrate, which serves to keep his interest alive.

An understanding of rule 4 allows us to continue our examination of "static" cuts. The simplest and most obvious static cuts are the beginnings and ends of sequences and self-contained scenes.

Rule 5: All scenes should begin and end with continuing
         action.*

Rule 5 is included not because its dictum is misunderstood or unknown, but because it is so taken for granted that it is surprisingly often forgotten or ignored. It is a corrective procedure, and its message is simple.

The beginning of a scene (this is especially true of scenes at the start of sequences) should never reveal an actor "preparing," or waiting, to act. An experienced director will, as a matter of course, give an actor the opportunity to "get into" a scene well before its usable beginning. If the scene is one of movement, the warmup may be as simple as walking across the set, getting up from a chair or sitting down in one, hanging up the telephone as though a conversation had just taken place, and so forth. The warmup serves to keep the scene "alive" at the point of the cut, to subconsciously suggest to the viewer that he is seeing a fragment of continuing life, not a staged scene with a visible framework.

An inexperienced director or one who "cuts in the camera" will often start his take just where the scene is meant to begin in the edited film, which allows the cutter no room to maneuver. This is especially troublesome if the scene is to be used in a dissolve. The only cure is to cut into the body of the scene, even if it means starting the dialogue under the end of the preceding cut.

A similar problem can arise at the end of a scene if the actor "lets down" immediately after his last line of dialogue, his last bit of business, or if the director is too quick with his "cut." The solution, once more, is to cut away while the scene is still "alive," either by cutting to another player's reaction, to the "kitchen stove," or to the next scene while overlapping the last bit of dialogue from the shortened scene.

---

*The word *action*, as used here, does not necessarily mean movement. Resting is an action if it is a part of the scene, as is sleeping.

You will be "saving" the director's film, and your "advanced" technique will probably elicit admiration. It will by no means be the first time that a last ditch corrective measure has been hailed as a creative cut.

Another common cut, seen many times in every film, is the "look off." Here is an example from *The Caine Munity:*

```
                    KEEFER
          There's just one more thing
          and you're finished. Climb
          that mast.

Willie and Harding look off, panicked.

LONG SHOT POV MAST FROM THEIR ANGLE

To Willie and Harding the mast seems at least a hundred
feet high. There is a tiny square grille at the top.

MEDIUM SHOT WILLIE, KEEFER, HARDING

                    WILLIE
                 (protesting)
          What for? A mast is a mast.
```

The "look off" here is quite clear. Less clear, however, is the last word in the writer's instruction: "Willie and Harding look off, panicked." There are situations where an actor's reaction to something the audience has not yet seen can be funny or effective. This is not one of them. Obviously, the panic (which is not the way the scene was played in actuality) would come *after* the shot of the mast.

This cutaway seems quite simple and straightforward, but a good sense of timing is required. The actor looks off, but just how long does he look?

The viewer, as a rule, will not accept the "fact" of a look until he sees the actor's eyes focus, or freeze, on something offscreen. At that point he too will look off, following the actor's gaze. By the time his own eyes have refocused, the actor's point-of-view shot (POV) should occupy the screen. To make the cut, then, we fix the frame in which the actor's eyes have frozen, add 3 or 4 frames more to give the viewer time to react and follow the actor's look, and then cut to the POV.

After making 50 or 60 such cuts, the routine will become almost automatic.

In the given example, however, *two* people look off, which complicates the cut. If they look off simultaneously, there is no problem—the two looks can be treated as one. But, if the two actors have different reaction timing, which is more than likely, where do you cut? Which actor do you follow? Do you cut on the first fixed look, or do you wait for the second?

The not-so-simple answer is another question: Whom is the viewer watching at the moment the cut should be made? If his attention is centered on the actor who looks off first, the viewer will follow his look, and that determines the cut, regardless of what the other actor is doing. However, if the viewer is watching the actor whose look is delayed, the second look now mandates the cut.

Another very common cut is introduced in this example—the POV—in this case the shot of the mast. The length of such a cut is a matter of judgment. If an audience reaction to the cut itself is expected, the cutter will let it run long—long enough, as in this example, to get a laugh started which will continue to build (it is hoped) over the ensuing shot of the actors' reactions. If the cut is too short, the laugh will die aborning; if it is too long, the laugh may weaken beyond the power of the reaction cut to resuscitate it.

The only rule for such a cut is a paraphrase of Lincoln's answer to the joker who asked him how long a man's legs should be. "Long enough to reach the ground," said Abe. The POV shot should run just long enough to deliver its message, and not one frame longer. Never give the viewer the opportunity to say, "All right already!" If the picture it presents is easily read, the cut can be as short as 2 or 3 feet. If, as infrequently happens, the cut is a repetition of an earlier shot with which the viewer is familiar, it might be shorter. On the other hand, if the picture is "busy," with its necessary point of interest somewhat obscured (the mast, with its array of antennae, etc., was such a shot), longer viewing time is needed.*

---

*The POV is one of the first victims of "nearsightedness." At each viewing, the POV with its loose dimensions, becomes more familiar and more dull, until it soon seems to run on forever. I have seen cutters "snip" a few frames off such a shot at each recut until it had virtually no presence at all.

If the cutter is really "with it," he will very gradually decrease the length of such cuts as the film progresses, even as the viewer's awareness becomes more acute and he begins to understand the film's characters, to think and live with the people on the screen.

Another POV shot is the *insert*—a cut of any inanimate object. An insert containing reading matter requires a special kind of judgment. Since there are great differences in viewers' reading abilities, a compromise is in order, although the laggard should be favored. The fast reader will gain greater clarity from a second reading; the slow one will appreciate a fully delivered message.

Each cut in the POV category is on its own, its length determined by the cutter's evaluation of its content. Timing is all. Errors come easily. The POV in whatever guise, insert, object, or scene, seems quite simple, but it can be a severe test of a cutter's mettle, and it gives the critical observer a good measure of his talent.

8

Trying a Little Harder

So far we have been considering action cuts made under perfect or nearly perfect conditions. But conditions are rarely perfect and not too often nearly perfect. A number of problems can raise their unattractive heads. Two scenes which ultimately will be cut together will often be shot on different days—sometimes weeks apart. Actors will have forgotten levels of intensity and the nature and speed of their movments.

For instance, in scenes shot for the exit-entrance cut, the actor may leave the first scene at a brisk pace and saunter into the next one, especially if the entrance scene has been filmed first. If an actor smokes a cigarette in the master shot, he will also smoke a cigarette in all the matching shots. However, only a superhuman memory could enable him to recall exactly how he raised the Marlboro to his lips, or when, how deeply he inhaled or how deliberately he exhaled, just when he lowered it to flick off some ashes, or just how long he paused before raising it to his lips once more.

Most actors do their best to maintain consistency, as do the director and the person especially responsible for helping the actor to match his wardrobe, his moves, and his demeanor, the script clerk. Unfortunately, the script clerk's memory is not perfect either, and her notes are sometimes inadequate. Besides, many directors refuse to allow their actors to be burdened with excessive detail, an attitude which I endorse. An actor who is conscious of the mechanics of his performance will usually perform mechanically. Freedom, spontaneity, and "being" go out the window if the player is required to devote more effort to matching his movements or "hitting his marks" than he does to making the scene come alive.

All this, of course, has to do with shooting, but it ultimately has a great deal to do with cutting, and the editor who is willing to try a little harder can indirectly help the director to get better performances from his cast. Knowing how much is possible, I refuse to allow the script clerk to advise actors about their action matching unless they specifically request it. When a conscientious script clerk objects, which often happens, my response is always, "We'll fix it in the cutting room." And we always do, even if it takes some doing.

The "doing" is where many inexperienced or inexpert cutters make serious mistakes. Confronted with a "bad" match at the preferred cutting point, they ignore the proper cut and search out a point at which the action matches. Now, the substitute cut may be technically perfect, yet completely undesirable, on at least two counts. First, it may still "jump" because it comes at an illogical and therefore unacceptable point in the scene. Second, what is much more damaging, it may diminish the dramatic thrust of the scene for the same reason. This leads to:

Rule 6: Cut for proper *values* rather than for proper "matches."

If the dramatic demand at a particular moment in a scene dictates a cut from, say, a full shot (A) to a close shot (B), the cut *must* be made, regardless of a bad action or position match. The cut can be accomplished in a number of ways.

1. Ignore the mismatch. If the cut is dramatically correct, it is remarkable how often the bad match will be completely unnoticed by the viewer. The important thing here, as in so many areas of cutting, is to know where the *viewer* will be looking. The mismatch which the cutter sees so clearly on the

Moviola is probably far from the viewer's center of interest. If he is watching the actor's eyes, a mismatch of an arm or hand will be ignored nine times out of ten. I have often been able to obtain a perfectly smooth change of scene even though the action in the two cuts varied widely.

In *Murder My Sweet*, I was faced with a closely related problem, a decided variation in lighting. Early in the film, Dick Powell, as Phillip Marlowe, is confronted by a menacing Moose Mulloy, played by Mike Mazurki. The tense scene was staged in a sketchily lit office at night. The only light source was the offscreen street lighting, dominated by a flashing neon sign positioned just outside the office window. Its on-off frequency of about 4 to 5 seconds was quite noticeable on the player's faces. The intermittent light effect was repeated, of course, in the "two-shot" and in the tight "over-shoulders." None of these key shots was played at exactly the same pace or with exactly the same sequence of movements. Although the light effect was started at the same point in each take, by the time the scenes had ended, the light effects were completely out of sync. Yet, a good deal of intercutting was dramatically imperative. Obviously, the on-off light effect created a problem.

I decided to "go for broke" and cut the sequence for its values, completely ignoring the light changes. I hoped for a miracle. It was not forthcoming. The lighting did *not* match. However, the scene played exactly as it should, and no one, then or since, has ever objected to the lighting anomaly. Over the years, this film, a prime example of *film noire*, has been frequently run for students. Not one has noticed the lighting mismatches, not even through several reruns. Only when they are specifically pointed out are they finally recognized. In short, the proper cut to the proper shot at the proper time is always the cut of choice.

2. If, for some valid reason, the required cut from *A* to *B* cannot be made, a cut into a close-up (*B'*) whose closeness omits the undesirable positioning or movement will often do the trick. If no such close-up has been shot, all is not yet lost. Here is a stratagem that has saved quite a few difficult situations.

The close shot (*B*) can often be blown up into a close-up on the projection printer. The quality of the print may suffer a little, but only the cameraman will notice, and he will probably accede gracefully to the demands of the scene.

3. If all else fails, the cutter can always precede the desired cut to B by replacing the latter part of the cut A with a close shot of its main center of interest, whether it be the speaker in the scene or an observer. The cut from such a replacement close shot, or close-up, will avoid the bad match, and although it might be criticized as a bit "cutty," it will serve its dramatic purpose.

To sum up, there is only one optimum way to cut a film, and the editor must overturn every stone in his effort to find it. Basically, it means showing, at any particular moment, that scene, setup, move, or reaction which most effectively delivers its dramatic message. Compromises may be unavoidable, but they should never be accepted without a battle. It is good to remember that the obvious is not always the best, and if one keeps trying, the ultimate solution can be superior to the original intent. Most important of all, the film's dramatic requirements should *always* take precedence over the mere aesthetics of editing.

9

Cutting Dialogue

Good drama* is never an essay, a lecture, or a straight narrative. It is always cause and effect, action and reaction, even when no physical activity is involved. A good dialogue scene is rarely a straight interchange of declarative lines or overt plot exposition, no matter how brilliantly written; it contains conflict, surprises, "twists," and "food for thought"—something for the actor, as well as the viewer, to ruminate.

In all good films it is essential that the characters grow or, to put it more accurately, develop, and such development is most effectively shown through their reactions either to physical crises or to verbal stimuli. These are the "moments of transition" which every actor and director looks for in the script's scenes, whether or not they consciously identify them as such. In addition, these are the moments of which every film editor should be especially aware, the moments which he should treat with special care.

Such moments contain two elements. Let us call them the "delivery" and the "reaction." Proper timing for each is of

---

*Drama is used here in the broad sense to cover all forms of theatrical presentation, whether tragedy, comedy, melodrama, musical, or other.

the greatest importance; where to cut *away* from the delivery and where to cut *to* the reaction may be most productively investigated in the context of dialogue scenes, since these are the scenes which, in the present state of the art, dominate most films.

First, however, let us examine a typical cutting breakdown for such a scene without regard to the niceties of the editing. Our example is a single five-page scene excerpted from the shooting script of *The Carpetbaggers* (Figure 4). It is not only a good sampling of several types of cuts, it demonstrates a point made on page 8 of Chapter 2.

The script was written by John Michael Hayes, at that time (1963) one of Hollywood's most highly regarded writers. It will be noticed that the five pages (the last half page is omitted because it is of no concern to us) are written as *one* master shot, even though the most cursory reading will reveal that a number of setups and cuts are required to properly develop the scene's several dramatic elements. (As the scene is broken down, it consists of 23 cuts derived from 10 or 11 setups—specifically, 4 close-ups, 3 two-shots, 2 or 3 group shots, and probably a reaction cut of Rina). The custom of writing dialogue scenes in master shots is the rule rather than the exception.

Our scene is "marked up" (admittedly more neatly than in the working version) with the director's cutting instructions for the editor who is to make the first cut. The cuts are numbered here for the convenience of analysis, but the rest of the directions, including setup identifïcation (e.g., 2 shot, Nev. & P.) and the slanting lines that indicate cutting points, are much as they were in the original breakdown.

On the whole, this is a straightforward sequence, and even if I had not shot and cut the scene some 20 years ago, I would, today, still probably break it down much as indicated. Of course, the proper cutting concept would have to be based on the cutter's knowledge of the characters, as learned from previously filmed material. Without that knowledge, the cutting sequence might be quite different, even though the cutter had access to the script. Characters as written and characters as played are often surprisingly different.

In order to furnish "live" footage for the dissolve into the

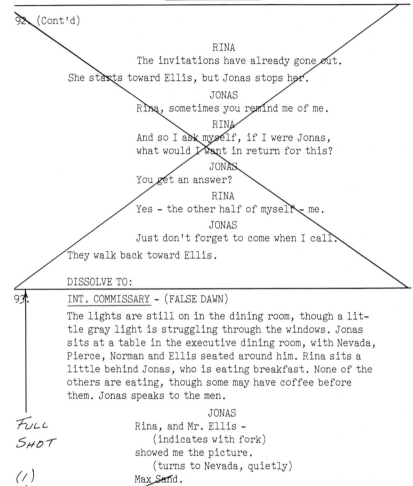

92. (Cont'd)

                              RINA
                The invitations have already gone out.

        She starts toward Ellis, but Jonas stops her.

                              JONAS
                Rina, sometimes you remind me of me.

                              RINA
                And so I ask myself, if I were Jonas,
                what would I want in return for this?

                              JONAS
                You get an answer?

                              RINA
                Yes - the other half of myself - me.

                              JONAS
                Just don't forget to come when I call.

        They walk back toward Ellis.

        DISSOLVE TO:

93.   INT. COMMISSARY - (FALSE DAWN)

        The lights are still on in the dining room, though a lit-
        tle gray light is struggling through the windows. Jonas
        sits at a table in the executive dining room, with Nevada,
        Pierce, Norman and Ellis seated around him. Rina sits a
        little behind Jonas, who is eating breakfast. None of the
        others are eating, though some may have coffee before
        them. Jonas speaks to the men.

                              JONAS
                Rina, and Mr. Ellis -
                    (indicates with fork)
                showed me the picture.
                    (turns to Nevada, quietly)
                Max Sand.

                              NEVADA
                The dossier, Junior. I put it to script.

                              PIERCE
                Is there something here I don't
                understand?

FULL
SHOT

(1)

2 SHOT
NEV & P
(2)
CONT.

                                                    (Continued)

Figure 4

THE CARPETBAGGERS   86.

93. (Cont'd)

CONT.

NEVADA
It's a private joke, Dan, between Jonas
and me.

(2) CONT.

Pierce retreats wisely. Jonas turns to Norman.

JONAS
Why did they withdraw your guarantee,
Mr. Norman?

C.U. JONAS

(3)

PIERCE
(interrupting)
Because he's an unprincipled, thieving,
son of a . . . .

~~JONAS~~ *NORMAN*
(mildly)
Let's deal in business, not per-
sonalities. Anger is for fools.

PIERCE
You call ruining a man's life
''business''?

2 SHOT
P. + NOR.

(4)

NORMAN
I'm ruining nothing! This is gambling!
Some days we win, some days we lose.

PIERCE
You're the richest loser I know.

Jonas watches the two men carefully, sizing up the two
men, and the issue. Pierce indicates Nevada eloquently
with a sweep of his arm.

PIERCE
Look at him - the biggest star you have
on the lot . . . .

NORMAN
The biggest <u>cowboy</u> star . . . .

PIERCE
Your bread and butter.

NORMAN
I make other pictures!

PIERCE
Art pictures! That don't make a dime!

NORMAN
They add culture and dignity to the
studio.

CONT.

(Continued)

Figure 4 (continued)

93. (Cont'd)

CONT.

(4) CONT.

                    PIERCE
They add three starlets a week to
your bed!

                    NORMAN
        (stands up - angrily)
I don't have to listen to this flesh
peddler . . . .

                    JONAS
Please sit down, Mr. Norman - Mr.
Pierce.

Pierce subsides and Norman sits back down in his chair. He
is obviously quite uncomfortable.

                JONAS (Cont'd)
Now. . . .
        (to Norman)
Why did you withdraw the guarantee?

FULL
SHOT
(5)

                    NORMAN
Talking pictures, that's why. I can't
sell The Renegade's Code for peanuts.

                    JONAS
(to Nevada)
Why didn't you make a talking
picture?

                    NEVADA
When I started the picture I didn't
think sound was here to stay.

                    PIERCE
Who did?

2 SHOT
NEV. + P.
(6)

                    JONAS
        (to Norman)
And what happens now? Do you throw
the picture in the ash can?

                    NORMAN
Maybe somehow we can salvage a
few pennies out of it. South
America - Australia - who knows?

2 SHOT
J. + NOR.
(7)

                    JONAS
That still leaves Nevada out in
the cold.

                    NORMAN
My heart bleeds for him. Truly.

                                        (Continued)

Figure 4 (continued)

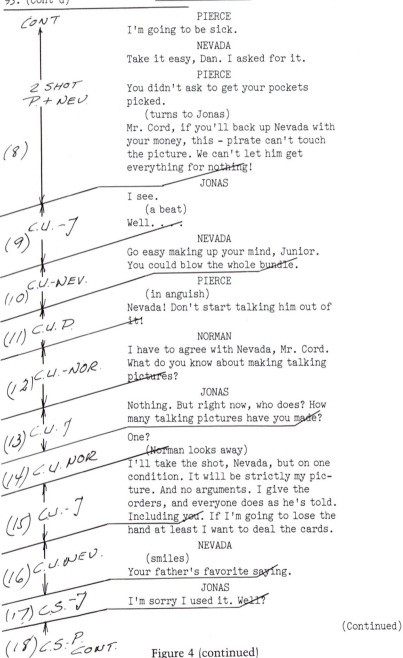

PIERCE
I'm going to be sick.

NEVADA
Take it easy, Dan. I asked for it.

PIERCE
You didn't ask to get your pockets
picked.
(turns to Jonas)
Mr. Cord, if you'll back up Nevada with
your money, this - pirate can't touch
the picture. We can't let him get
everything for nothing!

JONAS
I see.
(a beat)
Well. . .

NEVADA
Go easy making up your mind, Junior.
You could blow the whole bundle.

PIERCE
(in anguish)
Nevada! Don't start talking him out of
it!

NORMAN
I have to agree with Nevada, Mr. Cord.
What do you know about making talking
pictures?

JONAS
Nothing. But right now, who does? How
many talking pictures have you made?
One?
(Norman looks away)
I'll take the shot, Nevada, but on one
condition. It will be strictly my picture. And no arguments. I give the
orders, and everyone does as he's told.
Including you. If I'm going to lose the
hand at least I want to deal the cards.

NEVADA
(smiles)
Your father's favorite saying.

JONAS
I'm sorry I used it. Well?

(Continued)

Figure 4 (continued)

CONT

2 SHOT
P + NEV

(8)

(9) C.U. - J

(10) C.U. - NEV.

(11) C.U. P.

(12) C.U. - NOR.

(13) C.U. J

(14) C.U. NOR

(15) C.U. - J

(16) C.U. NEV.

(17) C.S. J

(18) C.S. P.
CONT.

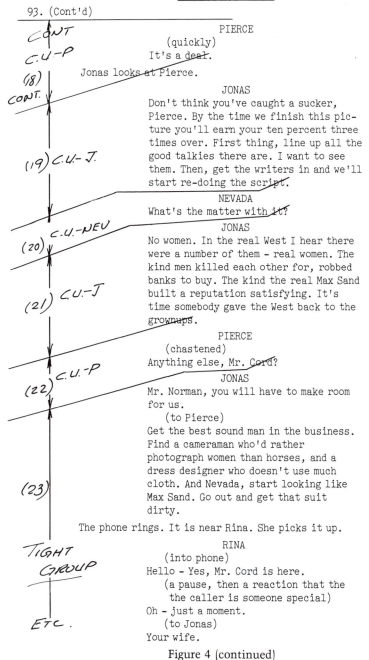

93. (Cont'd)

CONT
C.U.-P
(18)
CONT.

PIERCE
(quickly)
It's a deal.

Jonas looks at Pierce.

JONAS
Don't think you've caught a sucker,
Pierce. By the time we finish this picture you'll earn your ten percent three
times over. First thing, line up all the
good talkies there are. I want to see
them. Then, get the writers in and we'll
start re-doing the script.

(19) C.U.- J.

NEVADA
What's the matter with it?

JONAS
No women. In the real West I hear there
were a number of them - real women. The
kind men killed each other for, robbed
banks to buy. The kind the real Max Sand
built a reputation satisfying. It's
time somebody gave the West back to the
grownups.

(20) C.U.-NEV

(21) C.U.-J

PIERCE
(chastened)
Anything else, Mr. Cord?

JONAS
Mr. Norman, you will have to make room
for us.
(to Pierce)
Get the best sound man in the business.
Find a cameraman who'd rather
photograph women than horses, and a
dress designer who doesn't use much
cloth. And Nevada, start looking like
Max Sand. Go out and get that suit
dirty.

(22) C.U.-P

(23)

The phone rings. It is near Rina. She picks it up.

RINA
(into phone)
Hello - Yes, Mr. Cord is here.
(a pause, then a reaction that the
the caller is someone special)
Oh - just a moment.
(to Jonas)
Your wife.

*TIGHT
GROUP*

ETC.

Figure 4 (continued)

full shot (1), as well as to set up the scene and its personnel, certain "business," or action, not indicated in the script was extemporized when the scene was shot.

The number 2 cut, a two-shot of Nevada (Alan Ladd) and Pierce (Bob Cummings), enables us to accentuate a previously established "in" relationship between Nevada and Jonas (George Peppard). It also allows us to slide more smoothly, on Nevada's meaningful look toward Jonas, at the end of the cut, into:

Cut (3), a close-up of Jonas. This shot prepares us, gently, for Jonas' eventual domination of the situation and the people involved in it as it gets us back to the business at hand. Jonas' line, although spoken to Norman (Marty Balsam), brings an angry comment from Pierce, so:

Cut (4) is a two-shot of Pierce and Norman. A close-up of Pierce at this point, even though he is the speaker, would probably confuse the viewer, since Jonas, in the previous cut, has addressed Norman. The two-shot allows us to see the person addressed and to catch the interruption without confusion. This is the second two-shot which includes Pierce, and it serves to call attention to the director's responsibility for staging "cutting-compatible" setups. Nevada, Pierce, and Norman had to be placed in positions which would permit a two-shot of Nevada and Pierce and another of Pierce and Norman. Of course, these two two-shots could never be directly intercut without Pierce "jumping" from one side of the screen to the other, but either could be used when needed by cutting away from or to a close-up or, as in (6) to (7), to another two-shot of two different people. The third two-shot (7) of Jonas and Norman further complicates the staging and the cutting, but the previously stated rule applies also to this setup. If all this seems a touch complicated, rest assured—it is. Even experienced directors occasionally goof in such a situation.

To resume our analysis: cut (4) is a scene of bickering conflict, rapidly paced, with dialogue overlaps. Since no reactions of special import are present, it plays well in the two-shot. A group shot here would weaken the scene, and close-ups, as indirectly suggested by the writer's direction, "Jonas watches the two men carefully," would overstate the importance of the nattering and minimize the value of the close-ups to be used at the scene's climax. Cut (4) plays for a full page, some 40 to 45 feet at this rapid pace. The cut to (5) is then made in movement, on Norman's rise.

This kind of "action cut," involving dialogue, is quite common—and often quite troublesome. The actor rises as he speaks, but rarely does he do so at exactly the same point in each take (or setup) and rarely does the sound perspective of the two setups match. The best solution here is to cut for the picture match, allowing the dialogue from the two-shot to continue over the full shot. Even if the words do not synchronize exactly (and it would be a miracle if they did), the viewer's attention will not be sharply focused as it shifts with the action of the cut. By the time the viewer's attention is focused, that particular line of dialogue will have been completed and the next line, now properly that of the full shot, will have taken over. (An interruption here might be another complication, but more about that later.)

To resume, cut (5), a full shot, permits us to unruffle a few feathers, draw a deep breath, strengthen Jonas' position, and get back to the real business of the scene, while pulling away momentarily from what is really a secondary conflict, as we once again begin to build to a more dramatically sound (and inevitable) climax to the sequence.

With cut (6) we start to zero in on the real objective of the sequence, Jonas' takeover of Nevada's film, which, in turn, will soon impel Jonas firmly into the motion picture business.

Cuts (7) and (8) continue our two-shot buildup to what will be an extensive, rapid-fire intercutting of close-ups—cuts (9) through (22).

Cut (23) brings us back to earth. Associations and antagonisms which have become major story developments have been firmly established, and decisions, for good or ill, have been unalterably made. And to "springboard" us into the next sequence, the telephone rings, breaking the tension and bringing Rina (Carroll Baker) back into the scene.

These, briefly, were the cuts and the imperatives which led to them. Given the same setups and equal knowledge of the characters' earlier developments, half a dozen cutters, each assessing the sequence on his own, would probably cut it in much the same way, although minor variations would certainly occur. A television cutter would probably use more close-ups; an ''old-timer'' perhaps not quite so many. But in this breakdown one important element has been temporarily set aside. *Exactly where,* in each cut, does the cutter leave the scene and *exactly where* does he start each incoming cut? In this area, the cutters' techniques might vary considerably, and it is here that such variations might enhance or damage the tone, the pace, and the impact of each cut separately and the sequence as a whole. Let us now retrace our steps and examine each cut as carefully as we can with this element in mind.

Before we can properly handle an exchange of dialogue, however, we must first understand the grammatical nature of our language.* In speaking English, preferred usage generally requires that the subject be placed near the start of a sentence and that it be followed almost immediately by the predicate, whether simple or compound. The rest of the sentence, which might be quite long, usually consists of explanatory, enlarging, or modifying phrases and/or clauses. Certainly, in the majority of instances, the *sense* of any statement is manifest before that statement is completed. This leads to a common and sometimes unjustly condemned habit—the habit of interruption.

In most conversations, often even in well-chaired discussions, people frequently, sometimes constantly, ''cut in'' on each other. A conversation without interruptions may be polite—it is also, quite probably, very dull. Interruptions are not necessarily a sign of rudeness, but of eagerness. Anticipating the finish of a speaker's sentence, the listener is eager to respond, whether in assent or disagreement. Even if the listener remains silent, he will often react with a nod of approval, a grimace of doubt, or a frown of rejection well before the end of the speaker's statement, and although a spoken sentence may occasionally deliver a surprise ending, in the great majority of instances, this simply is not so.

---

*It is quite possible that the different structures of other languages would require different cutting techniques, but the principles to be discussed here, involving the use of English, can probably be modified by an intelligent editor to fit his native tongue.

In effect, whether with a verbal or nonverbal response, the listener usually reacts *before* the speaker has finished speaking—*and so does the viewer*. He too is a listener, and it is the viewer's awareness of the listener's point of reaction which properly determines a dialogue cut. With the foregoing in mind, let us more closely examine the cuts in our sample scene.

The cutaway from cut 1 should be made substantially as indicated by the diagonal line—somewhere in the middle of the word *Sand*. The viewer is aware of its significance because of an earlier scene, and he is now interested in its effect on Nevada. To linger on the cut, as many cutters would, is to lag *behind* the viewer, and that is a cardinal sin.

The average film viewer is a highly conditioned animal. He has seen hundreds of films and thousands of "situations." Rarely does he experience a truly original scene. His grasp of dramatic situations is usually quite broad, and his reactions to actors' lines very swift indeed. His tolerance of the ordinary should not be mistaken for stupidity. "Talking down" to an audience is a fool's occupation. It is difficult enough to "stay even" with the viewer—one need rarely worry about being "ahead" of him. The filmmaker must always try (although only a few will completely succeed) *never* to fall behind. That way leads to boredom, inattention, and failure.

At the end of cut (1), many cutters will allow the outgoing scene to run until they are sure the word *Sand* is quite finished. Since they do not, quite properly, want to risk cutting into the word, they give themselves a few extra frames for protection. This is good practice, as far as the *sound* is concerned, but there is no need to run the *picture* as long as the sound track. Picture and sound need never be cut simultaneously, and cutters who overlap infrequently are doing inferior work. In this particular example, it would mean that the cut has been made quite a number of frames *after* the proper *picture* cutting point, causing the viewer a moment of unwelcome distraction and an unnecessary lengthening of the cut (compare Figures 5 and 7).

The extra frames at the end of cut (1), combined with the three or four "empty" frames (see p. 60) at the beginning of cut (2), can add up to as much as a full second of "dead" time

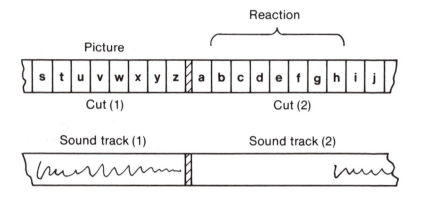

Figure 5

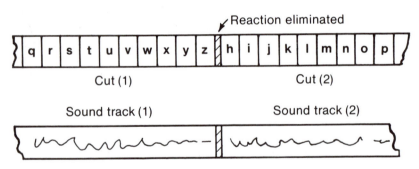

(Note: The frames of the film, as shown here, are purely suggestive.
In reality, many more frames would be involved.)

Figure 6

between the point at which the viewer anticipated Nevada's
reaction to Jonas' line and the point at which the reaction was
finally delivered. The "stall" is lengthened, and often when
the director or producer pronounces, "It's 20 minutes too
long. Cut it down!" the cutter, maintaining his "straight
across" cut at the end of (1) will clip off the beginning of the
reaction in (2). This will save some frames by bringing
Nevada's *verbal* response closer to Jonas' line, *but* at the

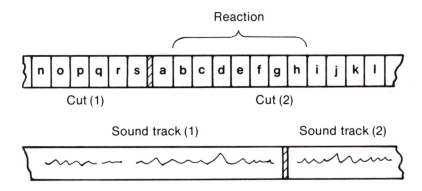

Figure 7

expense of Nevada's *visual* response, his reaction, which is, in classical film sense, much more important (see Figure 6).

For the proper (and much better) cut, see Figure 7. This "overlap" saves as much footage, and time, as the "straight across" cut in Figure 6, yet it retains *all* of Nevada's reaction.

Here, an equal, though not matching, amount of picture and track have been eliminated, while the important elements of the scene have been retained (Figure 8).

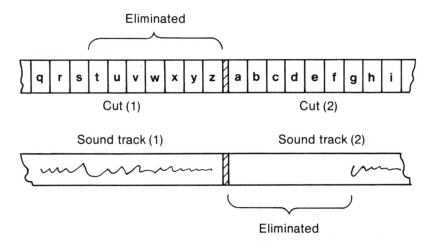

Figure 8

By cutting from (1) to (2) at the point where the viewer looks at Nevada, we are able to camouflage our cut without resorting to the "deception" of physical movement. The movement here is mental on the part of the viewer, and self-willed, since he wants to see Nevada's reaction to Jonas' line. If we hit it exactly, we present Nevada in a two-shot just as the viewer's eyes refocus on the scene, showing him what he wants to see and, incidentally, rendering our cut "invisible" (because it is made while the viewer shifts his eyes). We are able to show Nevada's complete reaction (preceded by three or four "empty" frames), we shorten the pause between the two scenes, and we keep the dialogue flowing.

This is the key principle for cutting dialogue. There are exceptions, but the great majority of dialogue cuts can be made after this fashion. The advantages are obvious—the cut "goes with" the viewer's awareness, it "hides" our cut, it conforms to rules 4, 5, and 6, and it enables us to maintain a tighter pace and a smoother flow.

The three or four frames preceding the start of any reaction cut, which I have called "empty" frames, are mandatory. The practice is based on the principle stated in Figure 3 of Chapter 6. It provides the brief moment needed by the viewer to focus on the new scene. If the cut were to be made just one frame ahead of the start of the reaction, the viewer would miss it, catching it already under way, a most undesirable effect.

To proceed, the cutaway from (2) is not made as quickly as indicated. There is a moment's pause as Pierce "retreats wisely"; then Nevada looks back at Jonas. The cut is made on the "look off" principle (see Chapter 7). We get to Jonas, in (3), in time for a slight reaction to the interchange in the previous cut, which is followed by the transfer of Jonas' attention to Norman. This close-up is also needed to separate the two two-shots, each of which pairs Pierce with a different actor (Chapter 9, page 54). The cutaway from (3) returns us to the overlapping principle of (1), especially since Pierce actually cuts in on Jonas.

Cuts (4) and (5) have been covered earlier in the chapter. The cut-away to (6) employs the overlap, since no time for thought on Nevada's part is necessary. The same is true for the cutaway from (6) to (7).

At the start of (7), time is allowed for Jonas to transfer his attention from Nevada and Pierce to Norman. Jonas probably has a brief reaction to Pierce's "Who did?" before he shifts to Norman. Here too, as at the beginning of all cuts, the three or four "empty" frames preceding Jonas' reaction, no matter how slight, must be included.

The cutaway from (7) is overlapped by the beginning of (8). Pierce actually reacts to "for him," so this extends his reaction slightly. His line is a near interruption of "Truly."

Cut (8) delivers the challenge to Jonas. Again, we use the overlap, as indicated, to cut to (9).

Cut (9) starts a series of close-up intercuts. The first, on (9), is known in cutter's parlance as a "timed cut." Jonas takes a moment to digest Pierce's last remark—his "well . . ." indicates the beginning of some decision that Nevada tries to forestall. Here the timing of the cutaway from (9) is instinctual. The cutter must guess at which point the viewer will look to someone for a reaction. A good cutter will guess right most of the time. The cut to Nevada (10) takes place during the look.

The cutaway from (10) is a natural overlap. We know that Nevada's line will cause Pierce some anguish, and we are eager to see his reaction in (11). From here on the cuts proceed at a rapid pace. The ends of all lines overlap, but the reactions at the start of the cuts are important and must be carefully timed and protected. There is one cutaway to a silent reaction of Norman (14). This starts as an overlap on Jonas' word "made?" His next word, "One?", comes over Norman's close-up. Norman's reaction to the question is obviously important, since it drives home to him, but really to the viewer, a very vital point, one which makes Jonas' forthcoming decision seem quite inevitable. As Norman looks away, we cut back to Jonas (15). Here, an extension of the "silent" part of the track may be necessary, since the full development of Norman's reaction and Jonas' awareness of that reaction is crucial. Such extensions of timing are often necessary and will be dealt with in a future chapter.

Cut (15) shows Jonas' full reaction to cut (14). It is important that he be aware of the effect of his "put-down" of Norman. The cutaway to Nevada (16) comes early, on Jonas' line, "including you." This is a key condition—the "gauntlet."

Nevada's reaction, by no means a foregone conclusion, is also important. Jonas' offscreen line is merely a restatement of earlier words put in terms Nevada can easily understand and accept. Nevada's answer, in (16), is a partial evasion, as well as a slight "getting even" with Jonas. Nevada is trying to retain his dignity even though he knows, as does the viewer, that he must accept Jonas' terms. The cutaway from (16) is an overlap, especially since Jonas (17) reacts sourly to Nevada's implication. His question, "Well?", is overlapped by:

Pierce, in cut (18). His quick reaction and line are matched by an equally quick overlap to (19). From here on, the end of each cut overlaps the start of the following cut, down to the end of the sequence.

Before concluding this area of cutting it is important to mention at least two exceptions to the quick overlapping technique. The first, already mentioned but not singled out, is not truly a dialogue cut, but it often comes up in dialogue situations; it is exemplified in Figure 4 in the cutaway from (2) to the close-up of Jonas (3). Although the dialogue in (2) has been completed, the viewer's attention is held by the visual interplay between Pierce and Nevada. The viewer must be allowed the time to absorb Pierce's important reaction of "retreat," at the end of which his attention is directed to Jonas (3) by Nevada's look-off. In (3) Jonas continues the interplay briefly, then changes the subject of the conversation and the direction of the scene. The movement from (2) to (3) is based on the "look-off" principle, but the cutter must know which "look-off" to look for.

The second exception is of a different and much more subtle nature. It concerns the posterior *elongation* of close-ups in a flow-of-dialogue scene, especially where the lines and the reactions deliver different messages. This is best illustrated by an example from Leo McCarey's *Love Affair*, starring Irene Dunne and Charles Boyer.

These two actors play star-crossed lovers whose long-awaited rendezvous at the top of the Empire State Building is thwarted when Dunne, hurrying across a traffic-crowded street within sight of the meeting place, suffers a crippling accident. Unaware of the mishap, Boyer assumes he has been "stood up." On her part, Dunne refuses to contact Boyer because she is now a quadriplegic.

In time, their paths cross, but under circumstances which still leave him ignorant of her physical condition. Piqued by their chance meeting and still very much in love, Boyer visits Dunne at her home. She successfully conceals her handicap by remaining seated throughout his visit. In the ensuing scene, Boyer's pride and Dunne's reluctance lead them both to avoid the truth as they recount their versions of the missed rendezvous. Yet this is the climax of the film, and it is mandatory that the truth emerge despite the fact that it is never voiced. Obviously, it could be done only through "attitude" or reaction, but not obviously.

Boyer and Dunne were masters of reaction. In this climactic scene, their "looks" had to belie their words, but in a most subtle fashion. These "looks" came *after* the spoken lines, being, in a sense, reactions to *their own words.* Therefore, it was necessary to stay with each close-up after the speaker's line had been completed, if only for a brief moment. Only then could a cut be made to the necessary reaction and response, at the finish of which would come another subtle ambiguous "look."

Since the viewer was completely aware of the situation, it was necessary to get him involved in a game of a sort—not if, since that was inevitable, but how and when will Boyer realize the truth. In this instance, the viewer participated in the game willingly, enjoying the delayed "looks" and eagerly anticipating Boyer's moment of truth. The beauty and genius of the scene lay in the fact that the denouement was brought about wholly by the "looks," or reactions, which followed completely plausible verbal deceptions.

Such scenes are rare because the teaming of such talent (including the writing and direction) is rare. But now and then a line or two of this nature does surface. The editing of such a sequence demands as much timing sensitivity as does the staging. The cutter must feel the exact point in the delayed reaction at which the viewer will look for a counterreaction, and a cut made at this point will inevitably be proper and smooth.

But cutting away from and to almost any reaction requires a finely honed sense of timing, which only practice can properly develop. However, a few hints may help, and in any case, this category deserves at least a brief consideration in its own right.

10

The Reaction Is What Really Counts

John Wayne was wont to say, "I don't act, I react." It was by no means an original phrase, and if it was meant as a self-assessment of his ability, he was shortchanging himself. At best, screen acting is a difficult art, whose subtleties often escape its critics; it demands great competence in all its aspects, of which, as the cliché indicates, reacting is one of the most important. In the theater, dialogue may be "king"—in films, the reaction is where most things happen.

Reaction is transition, change, movement—and movement is life. Reaction can reveal the birth and growth of awareness, show a quantum leap in levels of anger or of love, or discover to us the gathering of one's wits in thought or a change in attitudes or state of mind. It can express approval, doubt, or disbelief and do so in a universal language—without words.*

In comedy, it can range from the deadpan reaction of a Buster Keaton, through the wicked leer of a Groucho Marx, to

*Jane Wyman won the Academy Award in 1948 without saying a single word.

the screamingly broad distortions of a Jerry Lewis or a Martha Raye. In a more serious vein, it may range from the steady, almost sly look of a Spencer Tracy to the boldly stated responses, whether snarling or smiling, of a Jimmy Cagney at his best. However, whether obvious or subtle, no screen actor can claim to have mastered his art until he has complete control over all his reactions, and no film editor can claim to have mastered his craft until he can most effectively present those reactions to the viewer.

It can be argued that this is properly the concern of the actor and the director, and in a perfect world, this would be so. But unfortunately, in most collaborative efforts, whether in art or in politics, a great deal of time is spent in disguising lapses in taste or judgment, in fleshing out missed opportunities, or simply in correcting mistakes, and this is "cutting territory."

On the more positive side, it is rarely that a writer, an actor, or a director exhausts all the useful possibilities and nuances of even the finest script—which always leaves a "little something" for the editor to deal with. If an editor is willing to look for, and accept, the challenge, this aspect of the craft can be a good deal more rewarding and pleasurable than the amelioration of a film's mistakes. However, in both these areas, creative "handling" of reactions can be a rich and productive field.

Now let us "begin at the beginning"—understanding the *need* for a reaction, finding it, and then timing it. Writers are aware of the importance of the reaction as a vital element of communication. Some screenwriters in particular know that a good reaction can eliminate a lot of words, but full and accurate instructions are difficult to write in script terms. Besides, the actor and the director hate to be "written down to" as much as does an intelligent viewer, so the writer usually delivers his instructions in a conventional form. Here are three actual examples:

1. From *The Left Hand of God:*

> MARY YIN
> (a small shrug)
> Why not? Rice wine—and a woman—

2. From *The Caine Mutiny:*

```
                    WILLIE
                 (desperately)
              But, mother—
```

3. From *Walk on the Wild Side:*

```
                     DAVE
                  (grinning)
              How about upstairs?
```

A weakness of this convention is that it often leads to redundancy. Many writers are taught, or conditioned, to be playwrights—they feel that reactions must also be expressed through dialogue, as in

```
                     JEAN
                  (nodding)
              Yes—of course . . . .
```

But Jean is a fine actress, and her nod can say it all. In the first example, the "small shrug" *says* "Why not?" There is no need to verbalize it. A moment's thought will make clear how the line in the third example could also be eliminated, although this would have to be worked out on the set. As for the second example, the "desperation" was quite explicit in the whole scene; the instruction here was quite unnecessary.

A good director combs his script and carefully monitors his rehearsals for such obvious tautologies. And though most actors love their lines, the best of them have learned the value of acting through reaction and are eager to cooperate. Spencer Tracy, who could "read the lyrics" better than any actor of his day, was always happy to see one eliminated, and one of his reactions could replace a pagefull of words.

The great majority of reactions are easily identified. Consequently, they are often taken for granted. But even a procedure as simple as finding the start of the reaction requires close and careful examination. The Moviola does not necessarily tell the whole story, and often only the big screen will reveal whether or not the cutter has included the complete reaction in the film.

That reaction is not always heralded by a movement of the

facial muscles. The most subtle reactions may show a barely discernible "glint" or change in the expression of the eyes, especially if the actor is listening, as he should be, and not just waiting for a cue. The *very first frame* where the change begins must be marked, then preceded by the several "empty" frames mentioned earlier (see page 68, Chapter 9).

Obviously, the *length* of a reaction can have a decisive bearing on a scene's impact, but many filmmakers are not aware of how easily this factor can be manipulated. One quick example will illustrate the point.

Scene: A woman exits a building. As she nears the curb, a car pulls up and a man steps out. He wears a hat.

MAN WITH THE HAT
(quietly)

Hi, Molly. Hop in.

Close-up   Molly

Now Molly can react in a number of ways. We will examine the two extremes. First,

MOLLY
(without hesitation)

All right

Since there is no hesitation in Molly's reply or in her reaction, the viewer will assume that the situation is routine and that nothing especially dramatic is about to happen. Or,

Close-up   Molly

She hesitates, looking closely at the man in the hat. After a long beat, she speaks:

MOLLY

All right.

When the viewer sees Molly hesitate for a measurable length of time, he thinks with her, and a number of possibilities cross his mind. Is the man a near stranger? Is he someone she knows, but fears? Is he an ex-husband with vengeance on his mind? Is he going to "take her for a ride?" Or is he just a fellow worker collecting his carpool? Her eventual "All right," although spoken exactly as in the first version, will now have one of several possible meanings. Even the *sound* of her response will seem different because the viewer's imagination has been nudged into activity.

It *is* still possible to extract an audience input, and a good deal of that possibility can be contrived in the cutting room.

Let us examine two such manipulations which share similar solutions, First, in the previous example, let us assume that the scene was shot with the first version in mind. During editing sessions, it is decided to add a little suspense to the scene, either for comedic or for melodramatic purposes. (Such decisions are made more frequently than one might imagine.)

Second, a screen character is thinking his way through to an important decision. He is fully aware of his alternatives, which have been laid down in earlier scenes, and he makes up his mind expeditiously. However, the cutter knows that the viewer's awareness of the alternatives has been dimmed by intervening sequences, and he undertakes to give him more time to recall them to mind than was allowed for in the filmed reaction.

In both examples, extra footage preceding the actor's reaction is required, and such footage is usually available. It is that part of the reactor's close-up, immediately preceding his reaction, which shows him listening to the speaker who has supplied the "food" for his thought. As a rule, the listener does not move or react prematurely, and an extension of considerable length can be obtained from the "listening" footage.

An actor need not be "emoting" to supply the cutter with a reaction. Stillness also can be a vital expression (read, E.A. Poe's, "Silence—a Fable"). If the close-up comes at the point where the actor should react to a given stimulus, the very absence of movement can show a character "lost in thought." When the reaction finally comes, we know he is reaching a conclusion.

There are occasions, such as would be quite likely in the first example, where no footage for an extension is available. The cutter still has a trick or two up his sleeve. He can "freeze frame" the close-up immediately preceding the reaction (unless, of course, there is background movement). If the actor's move is not too sharp when his "live" action begins, no viewer will be aware that a foot or two of film has been "frozen" from one selected frame. The clichés "rooted to the spot" and "frozen in amazement" describe such a reaction accurately, and they have a most dynamic connotation.

Another alternative is to find a suitable reaction from another sequence in the film, which is not as unrealistic as it sounds. (I once found a usable close-up reaction in another film!) If the shot is close enough to avoid showing too much clothing (which might be different) and the hair is not dressed too differently (usually no problem with males), such a "borrowed" scene can be quite satisfactory, even if originally shot in a different setting. The background of a large close-up is usually unidentifiable at best.

There is an important lesson here for every beginner—one that every good editor has learned—*never give up.* If it is necessary to correct a fault, or if it is possible to improve the dramatic quality of a sequence, and the proper material is not at hand, explore *all* possibilities or invent a few. The odds that some workable solution can be found are so overwhelming that one should never stop trying, no matter how difficult the problem. Always remember that film is the art of illusion, and the most unlikely things can be made to seem real.

11

If You Can't Make It Smooth, Make It Right

So far we have discussed "smooth" cutting techniques—matches in movement, exit-entrance cuts, "lookoff" cutaways, reaction timing, and the use of properly timed anticipation in dialogue interchanges. However, even a superficial examination of almost any film will reveal a number of cuts which do not fall into any of these categories. They appear to be made arbitrarily and are seen, as a rule, in visual sequences such as fights, chases, contests, or scenes of suspense, in montage sequences, or in dialogue scenes which offer no thought transitions or opportunity for "mulling over" and where no essentially new information is being presented.* Such scenes, or sequences, are usually developments of established plot lines, goals, or characterizations, and their purpose is to move the story toward some minor or major resolution or climax.

This aspect of cutting, more than any other, tests the cutter's instinct for proper pace and timing. If his cuts are too

---

*I find it impossible to avoid the comment that this sentence aptly describes the total contents of the majority of today's films.

quick, or choppy, the viewer may be confused or irritated; if they are too long, the film lags, along with the viewer's interest. Each sequence of this kind presents its own special hurdles—rarely do they repeat themselves exactly—but a generalized discussion is possible through the use of hypothetical examples.

Let us examine the opposite of the precisely timed dialogue scene of substance, say, an argument between two characters in which maximum pace is desired. The basis for the conflict has been established earlier in the film, and additional information would be redundant; attack, defense, and counterattack follow each other at breakneck speed. Since the dialogue carries most of the dramatic burden and individual reactions are hardly subtle, many such scenes are filmed in master shots or, if broad movement over a considerable amount of space is called for, in a series of connecting master shots. However, let us assume that the sequence is lengthy and a point is reached where intercutting of swiftly paced close-ups will accentuate the verbal battle.

When the close-ups are shot, the mixer and the cutter will invariably request that the dialogue in each close-up be recorded "cleanly," i.e., without overlaps. Most directors will accede to this request. Overlaps would make proper cutting extremely difficult (although not impossible) and would "fix" the timing beyond the cutter's power to manipulate.

Cutting such a sequence entails a certain amount of labor, but few creative problems. The easiest, and best, approach is to use the *picture* as the guide.

An aside: With the exception of certain musical sequences, the cutter should work primarily with the picture in practically *all* situations. Even in dialogue scenes it is the image of the speaker, the listener, or the reactor which is important. The images change, interrelate, grow, or diminish; the sound track is, in a sense, an accompaniment, a continuous flow (even though its intensity and perspective may vary) much like the musical theme that underscores a sequence. The listener's hearing is continuous—his viewing is not—and the cutter's greatest efforts are always involved with the image.

This is not meant to imply that the creative possibilities of sound should be overlooked, although, aside from the compulsory dialogue and sound effects, they usually are. One of the weaknesses of modern film is that the creative use of sound has been ignored by filmmakers even more than the creative use of images.

Back to the argument: The cutter or director will break down his sequence diagrammatically, much after the pattern of Figure 4 in Chapter 9. However, now he will pay little attention to reactions. Instead, he will run the first close-up, say, of character A, up to the point at which he wants character B to interrupt. At this point, he cuts to B, allowing only the few "empty" frames to precede the start of the dialogue.*

In order to avoid cutting into A's line, two tracks will be set up, track a and track b, and these will carry the lines of A and B, respectively. This enables the cutter to run A's line to its completion on track a, while B's interruption runs simultaneously on track b. Player B's line, in turn, will continue in full on track b, even when A eventually cuts in on B. A's second line will, of course, be placed on track a, as will all of his following lines.

When the sequence is cut to the editor's satisfaction, he will get a "temporary dub," combining tracks a and b into one master track which takes its place in the work print. Tracks a and b are set aside for possible later recutting and as a guide for the final dubbing of the film.

There are minor variations of this technique for cutting rapid-fire, overlapping dialogue, but the one outlined here is probably the simplest, most accurate, and by far the least messy. It will also, with a little additional effort, accommodate additional interruptions from additional speakers on additional tracks.

The cutting of a physical battle, whether in the ring or in an alley, presents few new problems, especially if its setups have been well planned by the director. Normally, a fight has to be choreographed, much as a dance number would be. Anyone who has watched professional bouts on television understands how much "dead" time there is in most such contests. Many

---

*Most editors are good lip readers, and a cutter can save time and effort by cutting the picture without the accompanying sound, resorting to the "sound head" only if the actor's lips cannot be seen. When the cut is completed he, or more likely his assistant, will cut the tracks (a and b) to synchronize with the edited picture.

fights will feature no more than two or three solid blows in an entire 3-minute round. Even well-regarded pugilists have often saved their maximum efforts for the last 15 or 20 seconds of each round in the belief that a furious finish will make the greatest impression on the judges.

This should not be too difficult to understand. Unless he is a slugger who prides himself on his quick knockout (and there are few of these, especially in the lighter classes), the fighter must pace himself for a long battle. On frequent occasions he will rest during the "action," clinch while he catches his breath or move out of range while ostensibly exhibiting his "fancy" footwork. Although real, this does not make for a good film fight. Here the viewer wants constant action which can be clearly seen, and that means that the action must be carefully planned. In truth, unplanned action can lead to accidents and injuries which may delay shooting.

Fortunately, actors can rest between shots, most of which last no more than a few seconds. However, when a number of these short cuts are strung together to make a full round, the participants will appear to be the superfighters the viewer wants to see.

So in the great majority of film fights, each cut is planned and used to show a particular blow or combination of blows in a specific action routine. The planning, of course, is always done before the shooting, and the cutter's job usually consists of lining up the takes in their proper sequence, selecting the best angles for each separate bit of the routine, and then cutting them together by using the "action match" technique—there is always an overabundance of matching action to cut on. But if, for some reason, the director has overlooked the required action overlap, a cutaway to one of the "corners," the referee, or (less desirable) someone in the crowd can serve as the "kitchen stove."

Unless the cutter uses a shot of someone fully involved in the drama, a cutaway to an audience shot is not, as a rule, a wise move. The principle involved here is identical to that discovered in cutting early musicals. It is this: The viewer does not care to be told what his reaction should be by being shown a model reaction of our own choice. (The viewer is constantly manipulated, to be sure, but not in so brash a manner.) Once a "number" is under way, the viewer is the audience, and a cut to the filmed audience can be distracting, especially if the viewer's reaction and the filmed reaction do not coincide. Only if the filmed reaction is important to the plot (for instance, its approval of a "new" or substitute performer) is such a cut properly in order.

The same holds true for a staged fight. Only if the crowd reaction is an essential element in the story is it of any real value. Otherwise, it is wiser to let the viewer react to the fight and accept it as a real experience, exactly as one hopes he will with any and every other kind of sequence in a well-made film.

A street fight should also be carefully planned, for much the same, although more extreme, reasons. Although the dramatization of such a battle can be directorially very different from the more formal prize fight, the planning and the cutting follow the same pattern.

Since few, if any, blows, kicks, and so forth, of any weight actually land in a film fight, a few cutting tricks can help to manufacture "reality." Not all actors can "time" or "take" a punch properly. Let us say that in a full shot the puncher misses the intended target, his opponent's chin, by an unacceptable margin. On top of that, the receiver's reaction is a shade too late. If just as the first, in the full shot, should meet the chin we cut to a close-up of the "punchee" and see his head snap back as we hear a loud, dubbed-in, smack of the fist, the illusion of a solid hit can be made to seem very real indeed. In cutting such a sequence, I have often found myself wincing at such a blow, even though I knew that no actual physical contact had been made. Practically all film fights are a succession of such cutters' tricks—examples of the magic of screen illusion at its most convincing, if not necessarily at its best.

It is wise to withhold judgment on the effectiveness of such sequences until temporary sound effects are incorporated. The sound of the punches can make a world of difference in their appearance and believability, and although cutting in temporary sound effects demands a good deal of additional time and labor, it more than pays for itself at the eventual editorial runnings.

A first cut always has a great deal missing, especially in the area of sound effects and musical scoring. It is unfortunately a fact of the business that many directors and producers, despite their claims to the contrary, cannot truly judge a rough cut on its ultimate merits. But it is difficult for even the most experienced filmmakers to accurately visualize the film as it will look and sound after all the experts—the sound effects creators and cutters, the composers, the musicians, the rerecording and dubbing mixers, and the film timers—have had their turns at the film.

As an editor, I found it much easier to "sell" the directors, the producers, and the executives if I did as much temporary "cosmetic" work as I could possibly manage. It must always be kept in mind that they too have bouts of insecurity. Key sound effects and "library" music can markedly increase a film's dramatic, suspenseful, or romantic effects. As a matter of practical fact, the inclusion of temporary music is useful in another most important way.

David Racksin, that fine film composer, relates a typical tale of woe. "I have been told, 'We want to underscore this scene with a rendition of *The Marseillaise*,' but by the time the scene came out of the cutting room, I could only play the anthem's first two bars—if I rushed them." Racksin's experience is not too uncommon, nor does such snipping always benefit the film.

It is important to remember that a properly scored musical background has a very important effect—it serves to *increase* the apparent pace of most sequences. Therefore, if the cutter is moderately certain that a particular sequence will eventually carry a musical background, he must edit his film accordingly. This means he will probably opt for a pace slower than the one he expects the sequence will ultimately achieve. If he cuts the film to its maximum pace *without* music, it will probably seem hurried after the music is added. So he must keep this "otical" illusion in mind and resist the "itchiness" if the sequence, in its "rough" version, seems a touch lethargic. This is one more instance of the creative importance of an editor's instinct for timing.

12

Knowing Your Audience

The sharp-eyed reader may have noticed an occasional reference to the viewer or the audience. If he is especially discerning, he may have reached the conclusion that I regard the viewer as something more than a passive observer. He would be quite correct.

We have often heard or read some artist proclaiming proudly, if somewhat arrogantly, "I create only for myself." Overlooking its possible sour grapes aspect, this statement usually emanates from an artist who has not, at least not *yet*, caught the public fancy.

I am acquainted with no honest artist who does not want an audience, who doesn't pray for an audience, and who isn't bitterly unhappy if he can't attract one. Whether one is preaching, teaching, "illuminating," or just entertaining, an audience, especially a paying audience, means acceptance, and acceptance, in one form or another, is an innate desire in every human being. But beyond this, from a purely practical point of view, creating for oneself alone is a luxury no filmmaker can afford—unless he has the wealth of a Howard Hughes.

This does not mean that the filmmaker must pander to his audience. On the contrary, the creator must always "do his thing," but he must make it appealing. The ability to appeal, whatever the subject matter, separates the successful creator from the artistic failure.

Aside from the satisfaction of being heard, there is an important technical aspect to the creator-viewer relationship. The viewer is an observer, but he is also a reactor, and just as the filmmaker must understand the player's potential multiplicity of reactions, so must he understand those of his audience. Audiences are not fickle, but our knowledge of them is often incomplete. An artist who does not adequately read his audience can lose it as quickly as he once gained it.

It is essential to understand that there is more than one type of audience, and although an audience as a unit is curiously monolithic, one monolith may differ from another. A youthful audience, for instance, will accept information or entertainment in the areas of humor, sex, suspense, and social attitudes which an older audience might view with distaste. Further differences will be found between rural and urban viewers, between residents of the "bible belt" and those on the two coasts, between people of the deep south and the far north, and of course, between audiences of different social strata or cultures.*

Once an editor arrives at a good understanding of his audience, he can start learning how to use it. For instance, you are cutting a scene for a laugh—but what *sort* of laugh? There are many kinds of laughs, and an understanding of them is obligatory. If the most you can expect is a chuckle, you do not time your scene or play reactions for a guffaw. If you are letting out the stops in a sentimental scene, at what point does emotion become maudlin or sentiment turn into mawkishness?

The editor will find that previews offer him the best opportunities to study audiences. Previews are useful not only in the recutting and editing of a film—*objective* attention to audience reaction enables the perceptive editor to develop techniques for strengthening viewer participation in the film as a whole.

Once more I must stress the importance of *objectivity*. Many a film has suffered because of wishful thinking. Reluctance to properly evaluate or even admit an unfavorable reac-

---

*A film which is a hit in Los Angeles will often be a total flop in San Francisco.

tion has often precluded constructive reediting. Occasionally, an unforeseen reaction can be so completely negative that no remedial action can save the film, but in most instances corrective measures can be taken. These may involve a full or partial elimination of the objectionable material, a decisive change in editing, or a rewriting and reshooting of some or all of the offending scene or sequence. But the customary first course is an attempt at reediting—and quite often, if the scene's shortcomings are examined with complete objectivity, such attempts are successful.

One of the most important (but unhappily, most ignored) lessons to be learned from audience analysis is the value of silence. Very early in my editorial period I discovered that viewers are more attentive to silent sequences than they are to dialogue scenes.* This seemingly illogical phenomenon came as a complete surprise. I had assumed that the presence of dialogue would obligate the viewer to listen, whereas silence, which removed that obligation, would allow him freedom to indulge in occasional comments. Not so. When the screen talked, so did the viewer—when the screen was silent (except for possible underscoring), so was the audience.

Later, the development of recorders enabled me to tape preview reactions. The tapes generally confirmed my earlier findings. Even in substandard films, silent scenes commanded attention—as the cliche has it, "you could hear a pin drop"— while dialogue brought diminishing attention and occasional viewer repartee.

The silent sequence is most often seen in suspense films, whether they be mysteries, private eye or police versions, in horror stories, which cover a wide field today, in action films, also ranging broadly from gangster fare to Westerns, and in docudramas, seen almost exclusively on television.

Chase sequences, like fights, are always choreographed, either by the director or by his stunt coordinator. A knowledgeable director will plan his setups or angles to show every move or series of moves as he visualizes them. There will be few protection setups, and the cutter's job will consist mainly of finding the best action matches for stringing the cuts together. Later editing may require deletions of portions of the

---

*Every good mystery or suspense film demonstrates this point repeatedly.

action, which can be easily accommodated by cutting to the "kitchen stove," in most instances a shot of one or more concerned onlookers.

An inexpert or insecure director will cover himself with an excess of material. This places the responsibility for careful selection on the shoulders of the editor—a responsibility most cutters welcome even though the time and labor involved are multiplied by a large factor.

Chases usually feature a number of exit-entrance cuts, e.g., a car will exit one scene to be immediately picked up at the start of another which once more brings the car toward the camera or shows it moving off into the distance. Furthermore, chases almost always involve more than one participant, and many of the cuts are merely alternating shots of the pursuer and the pursued.* But when a series of two or more cuts of one of the principals is called for, the technique recommended for exit-entrance cuts (Chapter 6) should be applied. For instance, a car hurtles toward and past the camera. The next cut is a close shot of the driver, shot from inside the car. Here the windshield in the first cut assumes the role of the face and eyes in the earlier exit-entrance cuts. As the car's windshield moves halfway off the screen, the cut to the vehicle's interior will be completely unnoticeable. To the viewer it will seem that the camera simply passed through the windshield into a close shot of the driver. Try it. It works every time.

The cutaway from the interior will probably be made on the driver's look, or reaction, much like the average "look off" cut. If, on the other hand, a series of full shots is cut in sequence, the applicable cutting technique is similar to one used in editing sequences of suspense.

In a suspense sequence the most important ingredient, by far, is *mood*. Only rarely is character or plot development a consideration. The characters have usually been adequately developed and the basis for the suspense has been introduced. The stalking or hovering menace, whether human, animal, or extraterrestrial, is known to the viewer, if not always to the screen character. The cutter's obligation is to establish a mood which will convey the subdued terror or suspense to the audience.

*I say "almost always" because I once shot a chase in which the pursuer was unseen. The pursuer was fear.

The special technical aspects of suspense-invoking setups, lighting, and the use of lenses are, of course, the director's responsibility, but the juxtaposition of the cuts to obtain the greatest possible audience involvement is the responsibility of the editor.

What must be understood here is that it is the *viewer* who must be caught up in the mood. Showing a frightened actor will be of purely academic interest if the viewer himself does not feel the menace of the scene. If the viewer is to empathize with the character on the screen, he must be emotionally involved, even if that character is not yet fully aware of his predicament. Otherwise, the viewer may consider the character somewhat foolish when he finally reacts with fear to a stimulus which he, the viewer, has not yet accepted.

Fortunately, the cutter has a wide field of reference on which to base his cutting conception. Every person has, not infrequently, felt terror. The sound of following footsteps on a dark and deserted street at night has triggered a sudden flood of fear in all of us as children (and even as adults). The heart-stopping sense of an unwelcome presence in a darkened house as we enter it late at night is a universal experience. And parapsychological fears lie shallowly buried in the subconscious minds of even the most cynical unbelievers.

This potential for arousing the viewer's own emotional responses makes the suspense sequence the most sure-fire attention grabber in films. The cutter needs only to intelligently select and properly align the most effective shots or set up the most effective sound effects, most effectively timed, to have the audience reacting at his will. A shot of an empty street whose cleverly contrived shadows conceal hiding places for unnamed menaces or a suddenly billowing curtain in the absence of the slightest breath of wind can raise the hackles on all but the most insensitive necks.

Sound, whether direct or offbeat, can be most important. In one of Val Lewton's suspense films (possibly *Cat People*), a potential victim of an escaped black panther walks nervously through a cemetery. (The setting is obvious but effective.) Suddenly, there is a sharp roar, and an immediate audience reaction to the probable presence of the man-eater. Without pause, the sound turns into the harsh grinding noise of an automobile self-starter. Relief gives rise to nervous laughter, but the suspense, the certainty that the next such moment will be decisive, continues to grow. This incidental deception renders the panther's real attack, which occurs a short time later, even more terrifying.

The trick is to *never let go*—to pile effect on effect, to continually enhance the mood, to maintain peak viewer attention. A shot must be long enough to deliver its desired effect—it must never last so long that the viewer can start to analyze the components which make it work, not even for a brief instant. And it should *never* be repeated. No clever magician repeats an illusion at the same performance; neither should the film editor. A truly effective setup loses at least some of its punch the second time around. (This holds true for all shots, not only in scenes of suspense.) Just as "milking a gag" weakens a comedy scene, so repeating a clever shot weakens its total effectiveness.

As in other instances of arbitrary cutting, the selection, arrangement, and timing of the cuts constitute a "judgment call." They depend on the cutter's instinct and skill. The "feeling" for the viewer's attention span is all-important. Although, when cutting for suspense, reaction cuts are usually longer than normal to allow for the buildup and penetration of fear and/or terror, these cuts should stop just short of the point at which the viewer might become aware that he is being manipulated. Then, leaving the viewer at the height of his interest, each cut should be followed by another which will continue and, ideally, increase that interest.

It is, of course, essential that the cuts be aligned in optimum order. Since buildup is extremely vital, a close analysis of each cut must be made. An effective introductory cut may be of little use toward the climax of the sequence; a cut which may be useful in the buildup may produce a letdown at the denouement.

With this in mind, all the cuts should be lined up, analyzed repeatedly, and realigned where necessary, over and over again, until the cutter is completely satisfied that he has arrived at the best possible sequence of cuts. Only then should they be spliced together.

13

Dissolves: Why, How, and If

From time to time, certain techniques become fashionable and are considered "in" by filmmakers, including cutters. Every fad carries an inherent weakness which outweighs any possible benefit: A fashionable movement usually has one creator or trendsetter; all others are necessarily imitators or followers. In films, the fad is also self-indulgent, ignoring the viewer, who will usually react most favorably to the most effective technique rather than to one which happens to be chic. Beyond that, it limits the cutters' options.

In films, the fashion phenomenon has surfaced in a number of ways, e.g., in the craze for indiscriminate camera movement and in the use of dissolves. Camera placement, whether mobile or static, is the responsibility of the director, but the decision to use or eliminate dissolves is frequently in the hands of the film editor.

The function of the dissolve is mainly to facilitate transition. In its simplest form it can carry us from one place to another or from one time to another. In complex clusters, such as the Hollywood montage, the dissolve is the film-maker's "time machine," transporting the viewer instantly backward or forward in time and location at his will. In more sophisticated usage, dissolves aid greatly in the manipulation of pace and mood.

Before "talkies," most fades and all dissolves were made in the camera, a rather awkward and unwieldy operation. Shortly after the advent of sound, it became fashionable to eliminate the dissolve by cutting directly from the end of one sequence to the beginning of the next, no matter how extensive a transition was required. However, the development of the projection printer, with its ability to manufacture effects of all shapes and styles, brought the dissolve back into universal use. Much later, television rediscovered the straight-cut technique, and to a considerable extent, this fashion still persists. In both instances, dissolves were originally eliminated because of technical shortcomings and economic considerations, but the practice continues largely because of the working of the fashion syndrome.

At one time or another I have used all the techniques—I do not disapprove of any of them. I do, however, disapprove of the cutter who disregards suitability, who voluntarily limits his range by adopting only those techniques which are currently in fashion. There are occasions when the oldest cliché is entirely apropos, and attempts to avoid it lead only to circumlocution. Properly used, the dissolve is an asset; improperly used, it is a time-waster and a distraction.

Before discussing the different transition techniques, it might be beneficial to define the *dissolve*. This effect is not fully understood by many students or, surprisingly, by more than a few who certainly know their way around a movie lot.

A dissolve is not a *fade-out* or a *fade-in*. These two terms are adequately self-descriptive (although *black-out* and *black-in* might be more accurate). In the fade-out, always used at the end of a sequence or a section of film, the screen image grows progressively darker over a number of frames, usually 3 or 4 feet, until the screen is a dead black. The fade-in which follows reverses the process. Because of today's tighter story construction, fades are now rarely used, except at the start and the finish of the film. However, if the story breaks down into markedly disassociated episodes, fades can still be useful, giving the viewer a brief pause to catch his breath and gather his senses for the incoming section. Just as an unusually long novel may be separated into Book One and Book Two, so a film can be divided into discrete sections by fades—out and in.

A dissolve, on the other hand, has the opposite effect. It *connects* the outgoing and the incoming sequences, welding the two disparate sections into one. The second image does not displace the first instantly, as in a straight cut, but over a period of time, which may be as short as a quarter of a second or as long as a minute or more. The dissolve allows the two images to be seen concurrently, as in a double-exposure. As the outgoing scene dims out, the incoming scene grows correspondingly brighter until, at the end of the dissolve, the first scene has disappeared entirely and the second scene is seen at full exposure. There is never a period of blackness. In fact, the intensity of the exposure of the two scenes always adds up to 100 percent. In other words, when the printing intensity of the outgoing scene is 80 percent, that of the incoming scene is 20 percent. At the midpoint of the dissolve, each scene should have an intensity of 50 percent. And so it continues, until the outgoing scene registers 0 percent and the incoming scene 100 percent.

Leo McCarey enjoyed telling of the tyro director who asked for a few words of general advice before making his first film. Only half in jest, Leo answered, "If you find yourself in trouble, dissolve!" McCarey saw the finished film at its preview. "It was, scene, dissolve, scene, dissolve," he laughed, "from the start of the film to its sorry conclusion."

This rather sad anecdote illustrates one of the dissolve's remedial functions, one which, it is hoped, most cutters will have little use for. But it also serves to bring out a more positive point: The dissolve is of special value in welding two possibly unrelated sequences into one continuous whole when obvious juxtaposition of content or image is undesirable.

There is a vast array of dissolve patterns to choose from, of which the most exotic are seen in television commercials and film trailers. A spinning helix can wipe out scene *A* as it brings on scene *B*, or small squares of the first scene can be replaced in rapid, random succession by similar-sized squares of the second scene, until it occupies the entire frame. If something fancier is called for, the cutter need only ask. If he can dream it, the dissolve technician can bring it into being. For most feature films, however, the dissolves of choice are more sedate.

The most commonly used and, while still effective, most unobtrusive, is the *lap* dissolve. This was described earlier in the chapter, and it is the name used when both scenes are seen in their entirety while their relative intensities change in reverse proportion.

Following the *lap* in order of popularity and usefulness is the *wipe*, or *barndoor, dissolve*. In this effect, scene *A* is wiped off the screen, in any desired direction, disclosing scene *B*. Used as a "hard" wipe, i.e., where a visible dividing line can be seen sweeping across the frame, it can help to convey a sense of swiftness and action. For instance, in scene *A* a character walks off screen-left. As he moves, the entire frame is swept off the screen, right to left, at the speed of his movement, while scene *B*, showing the same character, or another, against a different background, is swept onto the screen from the right. This actually shortens the exit-entrance cut by a number of frames and imparts a feeling of speed to the scene transition.

"Soft" wipes, in which the sweeping line is invisible, are practically unnoticeable, but they impart a much more subtle effect than a straight cut could supply.

The lap dissolve, however, is the most flexible and, consequently, the most useful. The normal lap, or superimposition, runs 3 or 4 feet. (I prefer the longer version.) But for special situations, the length can vary considerably. For example, in *The Reluctant Saint*, Maximillian Schell, playing Joseph, a lay brother, is summoned by the abbot and told that his beloved father has died. As the camera moves gently into a close-up of the stricken Joseph, the scene dissolves into a shot of a tolling church bell, but it does not fade out completely. Instead, Joseph's image remains onscreen for some 40 feet until, with the shot of the bell still superimposed, it dissolves to a long shot of the front yard of Joseph's home. Only then does the shot of the bell slowly fade away, leaving us with a clear full shot of Joseph and his mother driving a donkey cart into the open yard.

This series of dissolves (three in number) over the long super-imposition gives the viewer a chance to experience Joseph's silent anguish while it establishes a mood which allows us to bypass his return home and the father's funeral. Into 30 seconds we compress days of actual time while still allowing the viewer to feel Joseph's emotions and to absorb the mood of the occasion.

On the other hand, a transition in *Give Us This Day* (*Christ in Concrete*) called for more speed and shock. As the leading couple expresses relief at the near attainment of a long-sought financial goal, the camera moves up to a close shot of a calendar, informing the viewer that it is October 23, 1929. Pausing just long enough for the significance of the date to begin to sink in, a quick dissolve (probably 2 feet long) discloses a moving tray of apples, the recognizable symbol (at that time) of the Great Depression. The camera pulls back to show the tray being carried by a shabbily dressed woman as she crosses in front of a group of men lounging listlessly outside the union hiring hall.

The double image of the calendar date and the apples throws us full force into the Depression, still a vivid memory in the minds of most of the viewers at the time the film was made (1949). Dramatically, shock was demanded here—mood followed slowly and inexorably. If the film had been made in 1979, I might have used the straight-cut technique, but probably not. Regular dissolves were more applicable in the greater part of the film, and a sudden change in style might have appeared to be self-conscious—a sin all filmmakers should avoid.

Whether straight-cut or dissolve, the main consideration here is that the cutter's decision should not be casually made. Each sequence transition should be carefully studied and the optimum effect selected while two considerations are kept in mind: (1) that each transition calls for the effect which best suits that particular situation, and yet (2) that the overall style of the film must never be disregarded. The two requirements may seem inconsistent, but the great variety of dissolves available make it quite possible to find a constructive compromise.

And remember, situations which permit experimentation will occasionally arise. Such opportunities should never be rejected. But the cutter must always make sure that the final choice in no way unfavorably disturbs the flow, the mood, or the content of the film as a whole.

A word of warning: There must be enough working footage in the film used through the dissolve to keep the scene alive even when the image is fading out (or in). In poorly made commercials one often sees an actor waiting for his cue to move or to start speaking as the scene fades or dissolves in on the screen. Unfortunately, one sometimes sees the same gaffe in a feature film, where it is far less excusable. The effect of such carelessness can be devastating, completely spoiling mood, effect, and the viewer's concentration.

This error is always the result of a slovenly approach to one's work and can easily be avoided by giving dissolves the same care one would expend on any other cutting problem.

Dissolves are essential, of course, in the construction of montage, but this field requires a chapter to itself.

14

Editing—Simple And Pure

Editing is to cutting as architecture is to bricklaying—one is an art; the other is a craft. Not all architects are brilliant, nor is all architecture high art, but at its best it is undeniably creative. So is editing. In the realm of film, however, the ''architect'' may also be the ''bricklayer'' or, more properly, vice versa: The cutter may be the editor, but not necessarily so.

It must be understood that the editing or reediting of a film is not always standard procedure. Some scripts are well written, and minor changes, if any, are made during production. Scenes are well staged, well acted, and well shot. The cutter's job is then relatively simple; he needs only to join the relevant portions of the selected takes together in the most efficient and properly paced manner.

In a fair percentage of cases, however, it is not quite that easy and not nearly so straightforward. Especially on the more ambitious projects, problems, not always unforeseen, will arise. Films such as *Reds, Lawrence of Arabia, Gone With the Wind, Dr. Zhivago,* or my own *The Young Lions* carry such complex plots and are inhabited by so many characters that intelligent story decisions cannot always be made at the script stage or even at the shooting stage. Some scenes may be shot "on spec," and the final judgment as to their worth may be deferred until after the first cut has been viewed. Then the work begins. It is by no means unusual for that work to take two, three, or even four times as long as the actual shooting.

When deletion starts, the speculative scenes or sequences are not always the first to go. Contributions of the director and/or the actors may have changed values, relative importance, or even story direction during the course of photography. Even everybody's favorite scene (in the script) may turn out to be expendable on the screen. An opening scene, for instance, written for purely expository purposes, may turn out to be redundant if the characters, due to brilliant interpretation on the set, have been more fully developed throughout the film than they had originally been visualized. Or, not infrequently, a realignment of a scene may help to clarify a circuitous plot or a fuzzy character.

All this is not too different from the contribution of a literary editor whose authors have a leaning toward long-windedness.* But there is one marked dissimilarity. Film is not as malleable or as cheap as print. If a segment of a novel is deleted, a sentence or two may be all that is needed to fashion a proper bridge or transition. In films, the equivalent of that sentence or two will probably not have been shot, and retakes or added scenes cost many thousands of dollars. The saving of those thousands of dollars can sometimes be accomplished by the application of some ingenuity, at the least, or creativity, at best. Let us now consider a few examples of the different types of "editing," as opposed to "cutting," that may be required.

The first example is a segment from the early pages of *The End of the Affair*, Lenore Coffee's screenplay of the novel by Graham Greene. The changes in this short scene do not result in any measurable shortening of its length, and the material was all at hand from the original shooting. However, since the continuity was now altered, special care had to be taken to ensure a smooth, noncontradictory flow of images.

Figure 9 shows the scene as it appeared in the shooting script. (It will be noted that it was written as a master scene.) Figure 10 shows the same pages marked out for the new align-

---

*Thomas Wolfe is perhaps the best-known example of such a writer, and currently, James Clavell freely confesses that his editor is his "Life-saver."

ment; i.e., the sections which follow each other are designated (1), (2), (3), etc. Figure 11 presents the rearranged scene, with the cuts that made the rearrangement possible now indicated in script terms. The apparent increase in length is due to the insertion of the angle descriptions. In reality, the scene was shortened by a few seconds, but that was not the purpose of the changes.

First, study Figure 9.

Then, study the changes as indicated in Figure 10.

Since the purposes of the changes are by no means clearly evident on even careful examination, a rationalization is in order.

The chief aim of the realignment is to break up Bendrix's continuing speech on page 6 [(numbers (2), (4), and the first part of (6)]. This operation is needed to allow more give and take in the dialogue, to eliminate the image of Henry standing dumbly (and unnaturally) while Bendrix ambles through his lines, his reactions, and his transitions, and to camouflage the expository nature of the last part of Bendrix's speech (6).

Now, the rationalization in detail:

Page 5 of the insert stands as is—no changes are needed. It quite satisfactorily establishes the tension for the moments that follow.

On page 6 it seemed more honest to have Henry present the letter promptly rather than beat about the bush with his oblique reference to some obscure problem. As it stands in the original, Bendrix takes Henry's line (3) in stride ("I'm sorry"), as if he knows exactly what Henry is talking about. As far as the viewer is concerned, of course, he does not. We find out as the scene progresses that Henry's only purpose in bringing Bendrix into his home is to discuss with him the letter and the situation which gave it birth. To show Henry behaving like a bashful schoolboy before getting to the point works against the character.

Instead, the new alignment allows us to understand, as Bendrix reads the opening paragraph of the letter, what Henry has on his mind. Now speech (3) has an altogether different thrust. It is no longer a puzzling circumlocution, but rather a somewhat indirect allusion to the reason for the letter's intent; he mistrusts his wife—and it hurts.

6.   HENRY'S STUDY

As Henry comes in he pokes up the fire until it burns
brightly. It is a quiet, studious room, with leather
chairs and a great many uniform volumes of books on the
shelves and an oil painting or two. Bendrix comes in
and stands looking about the room.

                    BENDRIX
           I don't think I've seen this room
           before.

                    HENRY
           It's my study.

                    BENDRIX
           Spend much time in it?

                    HENRY
              (leaving the fire)
           A good deal. That is, whenever
           Sarah's out.

Henry stands irresolutely. Bendrix looks at him with a
friendly, mocking air.

                    BENDRIX
           What's troubling you, Henry?

                    HENRY
              (with sudden helplessness)
           Bendrix -- I'm afraid.

                    BENDRIX
           What is it you're afraid of?

Henry crosses to his desk and picks up a letter lying
face down. His face is filled with disgust.

                    HENRY
           I've always thought the worst thing a
           man could do -- the very worst --

He is unable to continue. Bendrix replies smoothly ---

                    BENDRIX
           You know you can trust me, Henry.

                    Figure 9

6

> HENRY
> I haven't done anything about it, but
> this letter has sat on my desk remind-
> ing me. It seems so silly, doesn't it,
> that I can trust Sarah absolutely not
> to read it, though she comes in here a
> dozen times a day, and yet I can't
> trust ---- She's out for a walk now - a
> walk, Bendrix...

He breaks off with a gesture of despair.

> BENDRIX
> I'm sorry.

> HENRY
> They always say, don't they, that a
> husband is the last person to know ---
> (thrusts letter toward Bendrix)
> Read it, Bendrix.

Bendrix takes the letter with no inkling of its contents,
and increasing surprise as he reads it aloud.

> BENDRIX
> (reading)
> 'In reply to your inquiry, I would sug-
> gest you employ the services of a fellow
> called Savage, 159 Vigo Street. From
> all reports he has the reputation of
> being both able and discreet ---'
> (he reads on a bit, then looks
>   up, genuinely startled)
> You mean that you want a private detec-
> tive to follow Sarah?
> (Henry nods)
> Really, Henry, you surprise me. One of
> His Majesty's most respected Civil
> Servants ...
> (Bendrix looks incredulous)
> Funny - I imagined your mind was as
> neatly creased as your trousers.

> HENRY
> I thought when I saw you in the
> Square tonight that if I told you,
> and you laughed at me, I might be

CONTINUED:

Figure 9 (continued)

                    HENRY (cont.)
          able to burn the letter.
                    (hopefully)
          You do think that I'm a fool, don't you?

                    BENDRIX
          Oh, no, I don't think you're a fool,
          Henry. After all, Sarah's human.

                    HENRY
          You mean, you think it's possible?

                    BENDRIX
                    (shrugs)
          Why not go and see this Mr. Savage --
          then you'd know.

Henry stands indecisively, the letter in his hand.

                    HENRY
          And I always thought you were a
          special friend of hers, Bendrix...

                    BENDRIX
          I only said it was possible - I
          didn't say anything about Sarah.

                    HENRY
          I know. I'm sorry.
                    (with a burst of feeling)
          You can't think what I've been through
          all these months. I never know where
          she is or what she is doing. She's
          away at all hours, Bendrix - and no
          explanation

                    BENDRIX
                    (almost impatiently)
          Then see Mr. Savage.

                    HENRY
          But just think - sitting there in
          front of a desk, in a chair all the
          other jealous husbands have sat in --

Henry gives a shudder of distaste. Bendrix looks at him
with an odd smile.

                    BENDRIX
          Why not let me go, Henry?

                    Figure 9 (continued)

6.   HENRY'S STUDY

As Henry comes in he pokes up the fire until it burns
brightly. It is a quiet, studious room, with leather
chairs and a great many uniform volumes of books on the
shelves and an oil painting or two. Bendrix comes in
and stands looking about the room.

                    BENDRIX
          I don't think I've seen this room
          before.

                    HENRY
          It's my study.

                    BENDRIX
          Spend much time in it?

                    HENRY
               (leaving the fire)
          A good deal. That is, whenever
          Sarah's out.

Henry stands irresolutely. Bendrix looks at him with a
friendly, mocking air.

                    BENDRIX
          What's troubling you, Henry?

                    HENRY
               (with sudden helplessness)
          Bendrix -- I'm afraid.

                    BENDRIX
          What is it you're afraid of?

Henry crosses to his desk and picks up a letter lying
face down. His face is filled with disgust.

                    HENRY
          I've always thought the worst thing a
          man could do -- the very worst --

He is unable to continue. Bendrix replies smoothly ---

                    BENDRIX
          You know you can trust me, Henry.

Figure 10

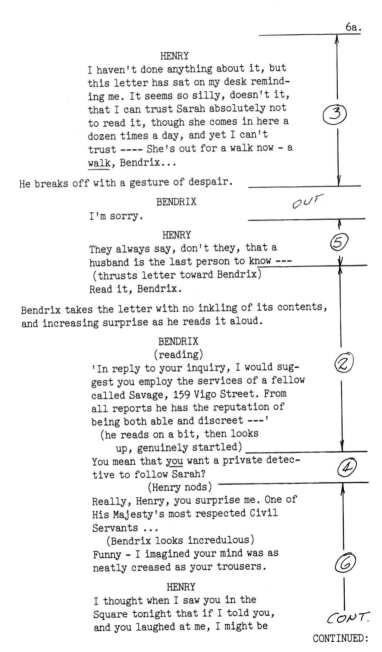

6a.

HENRY

I haven't done anything about it, but
this letter has sat on my desk remind-
ing me. It seems so silly, doesn't it,
that I can trust Sarah absolutely not
to read it, though she comes in here a
dozen times a day, and yet I can't
trust ---- She's out for a walk now - a
walk, Bendrix...

③

He breaks off with a gesture of despair.

BENDRIX   OUT

I'm sorry.

HENRY

They always say, don't they, that a
husband is the last person to know ---
(thrusts letter toward Bendrix)
Read it, Bendrix.

⑤

Bendrix takes the letter with no inkling of its contents,
and increasing surprise as he reads it aloud.

BENDRIX
(reading)

'In reply to your inquiry, I would suggest you employ the services of a fellow
called Savage, 159 Vigo Street. From
all reports he has the reputation of
being both able and discreet ---'
(he reads on a bit, then looks
up, genuinely startled)

②

You mean that you want a private detec-
tive to follow Sarah?
(Henry nods)
Really, Henry, you surprise me. One of
His Majesty's most respected Civil
Servants ...
(Bendrix looks incredulous)
Funny - I imagined your mind was as
neatly creased as your trousers.

④

⑥

HENRY

I thought when I saw you in the
Square tonight that if I told you,
and you laughed at me, I might be

CONT.

CONTINUED:

Figure 10 (continued)

7a.
CONT.

> HENRY (cont.)
> able to burn the letter.
> > (hopefully)
> You do think that I'm a fool, don't you?

⑥

> BENDRIX
> Oh, no, I don't think you're a fool,
> Henry. After all, Sarah's human.

> HENRY
> You mean, you think it's possible?

> BENDRIX
> > (shrugs)
> Why not go and see this Mr. Savage --
> then you'd know.

⑧

Henry stands indecisively, the letter in his hand.   *OUT*

> HENRY
> And I always thought you were a
> special friend of hers, Bendrix...

> BENDRIX
> I only said it was possible - I
> didn't say anything about Sarah.

⑦

> HENRY
> I know. I'm sorry.
> > (with a burst of feeling)
> You can't think what I've been through
> all these months. I never know where
> she is or what she is doing. She's
> away at all hours, Bendrix - and no
> explanation

> BENDRIX
> > (almost impatiently)
> Then see Mr. Savage.

OUT

> HENRY
> But just think - sitting there in
> front of a desk, in a chair all the
> other jealous husbands have sat in --

Henry gives a shudder of distaste. Bendrix looks at him
with an odd smile.

⑨

> BENDRIX
> Why not let me go, Henry?

CONT.

Figure 10 (continued)

As a consequence, Bendrix's next line (4) does not seem so gratuitous. Even though the line is a question, he is not guessing, but making a positive comment.

Line (5) is a further development of Henry's sense of guilt and impropriety; again, not arbitrarily made, but in shamed answer to Bendrix's attacking question.

Now (in 6) Bendrix has had time to put his thoughts, reactions, and emotions into place, and he continues the scene with a mocking chiding of Henry—a chiding that is really expository. But though the line tells us a good deal about Henry, its expository nature is concealed by its more apparent purpose—a gentle put-down and a quick puncturing of Henry's mounting self-pity. As Henry's answer indicates, this is exactly what he has been looking for as a way out of a degrading situation. It also gets the conversation back to a more hopeful direction (for Henry), only to have him jolted once more by Bendrix's cynicism ("After all, Sarah's human").

The changes on page 7 are made, first, to make Henry's protest—"And I always thought you were a special friend of hers, Bendrix . . ."—come in answer to Bendrix's cynical shrug rather than to the suggestion that he see Mr. Savage and, second, to diminish the line's expository nature by making it a deeper expression of the drama of the scene. In other words, Henry's reply seems a logical reaction to Bendrix's shrug rather than a line inserted only to inform us that Bendrix knows Sarah.

The third purpose of the realignment is to eliminate Bendrix's "impatient" urging. Too much insistence on his part should make Henry suspicious, something both we and Bendrix are clever enough to avoid.

Figure 11 should now be read through nonclinically in order to absorb the flow of the realigned scene. At first reading the effect of the changes may seem slight, but as indicated in the foregoing paragraphs, they have considerable bearing on the believability of the scene and on the honesty of the characters in it.

6.   HENRY'S STUDY

        As Henry comes in he pokes up the fire until it burns
        brightly. It is a quiet, studious room, with leather
        chairs and a great many uniform volumes of books on the
        shelves and an oil painting or two. Bendrix comes in
        and stands looking about the room.

                            BENDRIX
                  I don't think I've seen this room
                  before.

                            HENRY
                  It's my study.

                            BENDRIX
                  Spend much time in it?

                            HENRY
                        (leaving the fire)
                  A good deal. That is, whenever
                  Sarah's out.

        Henry stands irresolutely. Bendrix looks at him with a
        friendly, mocking air.

                            BENDRIX
                  What's troubling you, Henry?

                            HENRY
                        (with sudden helplessness)
                  Bendrix -- I'm afraid.

                            BENDRIX
                  What is it you're afraid of?

        Henry crosses to his desk and picks up a letter lying
        face down. His face is filled with disgust.

                            HENRY
                  I've always thought the worst thing a
                  man could do -- the very worst --

        He is unable to continue. Bendrix replies smoothly ---

                            BENDRIX
                  You know you can trust me, Henry.

                        Figure 11

7.   CLOSE-UP   HENRY

He thrusts the letter toward Bendrix,

                          HENRY
                   Read it, Bendrix.

8.   CLOSE-UP   BENDRIX

He takes the letter with no inkling of its contents.
He reads it aloud with increasing surprise.

                         BENDRIX
                         (reading)
                'In reply to your inquiry, I would sug-
                gest you employ the services of a fellow
                called Savage, 159 Vigo Street. From
                all reports he has the reputation of
                being both able and discreet ---'
                   (he reads on a bit, then looks
                       up, startled)

9.   CLOSE-UP   HENRY

                          HENRY
                I haven't done anything about it, but
                this letter has sat on my desk remind-
                ing me. It seems so silly, doesn't it,
                that I can trust Sarah absolutely not
                to read it, though she comes in here a
                dozen times a day, and yet I can't
                trust ---- She's out for a walk now - a
                walk, Bendrix...
                       (breaks off with a
                       gesture of despair)

10.   CLOSE-UP   BENDRIX

                         BENDRIX
                You mean that you want a private detec-
                tive to follow Sarah?

11.   CLOSE-UP   HENRY

                          HENRY
                They always say, don't they, that a
                husband is the last person to know ---

                   Figure 11 (continued)

7b.

12.   TWO SHOT   BENDRIX AND HENRY

                              BENDRIX
                    Really, Henry, you surprise me. One of
                    His Majesty's most respected Civil
                    Servants...
                        (Bendrix looks incredulous)
                    Funny - I imagined your mind was as
                    neatly creased as your trousers.

                              HENRY
                    I thought when I saw you in the
                    Square tonight that if I told you,
                    and you laughed at me, I might be
                    able to burn the letter.
                              (hopefully)
                    You do think that I'm a fool, don't you?

                              BENDRIX
                    Oh, no, I don't think you're a fool,
                    Henry. After all, Sarah's human.

                              HENRY
                    You mean, you think it's possible?

          Bendrix shrugs.

13.   CLOSE-UP   HENRY

                              HENRY (cont.)
                    And I always thought you were a
                    special friend of hers, Bendrix....

14.   CLOSE-UP   BENDRIX

                              BENDRIX
                    I only said it was possible - I
                    didn't say anything about Sarah.

15.   CLOSE-UP   HENRY

                              HENRY
                    I know. I'm sorry.
                        (with a burst of feeling)
                    You can't think what I've been through
                    all these months. I never know where
                    she is or what she is doing. She's
                    away at all hours, Bendrix - and no
                    explanation...

                         Figure 11 (continued)

16.   CLOSE-UP   BENDRIX

                              BENDRIX
                    Why not go and see this Mr. Savage
                    --then you'd know.

17.   TWO SHOT   HENRY AND BENDRIX

                              HENRY
                    But just think - sitting there in
                    front of a desk, in a chair all the
                    other jealous husbands have sat in --

Henry gives a shudder of distaste. Bendrix looks at him
with an odd smile.

                              BENDRIX
                    Why not let me go, Henry?

                    Figure 11 (continued)

15

More of the Same

The next editing example is a scene from *A Walk on the Wild Side*, a film written by a number of writers, based on Nelson Algren's novel of the same name.

In this scene, the problem is twofold: first, to shorten it as much as possible, since too much time is taken to deliver its simple message, and second, to eliminate as much as possible of its mawkish flavor. Figure 12 presents the scene as written.

Figure 13, which follows, indicates the proposed cuts. In this instance, the alignment of the retained portions follows the original sequence, with deletions accomplished by cutting to angles that were originally shot. The reedited version is more than one-third shorter and immeasurably less maudlin.

The first deletion, on page 8b of the insert (Figure 11), gets Amy directly to the point, which is consistent with her character and with her attitude toward Dove.

Amy's line in (2) is pure exposition, but its nature is camouflaged to some extent by using the information as a basis for making the scene one of conflict.

13   FULL SHOT   INT. GERARD SUNROOM   DAY

As Dove enters, the object that first pulls his eyes with
irresistible power is the painting over the fireplace.
The painting is impressionistic, unsparingly real -- a
face wreathed in some mysterious and indefinable pain.
Dove stares at it in confusion. Suddenly Eva breaks
the spell.

                              EVA
                   It's a self-portrait.

                              DOVE
                   It -- it looks like Hallie --
                   and yet it doesn't.

He turns toward Amy with an abrupt, pleading urgency.

                         DOVE (cont.)
                   Miss Gerard, where is she?

                              AMY
                           (flatly)
                   My condolences on the death of
                   your father.

                              DOVE
                         (desperately)
                   Where is Hallie, Ma'am?

                              AMY
                   Her whereabouts are no business
                   of yours.

                              EVA
                   Amy...!

                              AMY
                        (ignoring her)
                   My niece is not for you, Mister
                   Linkhorn. Hallie was born and raised in
                   Europe -- in Paris. She's had everything
                   -- known everything. Beside her, what
                   are you? An uneducated dirt farmer.

                              DOVE
                        (fighting back)
                   I'm through with farming. I
                   mean to look into other things....

                         Figure 12

Amy makes a scoffing noise.

> DOVE (cont.)
> Pa used to say no man can be
> sure of his callin' till he's
> thirty. That's when Christ
> got started.

> AMY
> Sounds like Fitz Linkhorn, all right.

> DOVE
> (bursting out)
> Tell me where Hallie is, Miss Gerard.

A flush of anger touches Amy's cheek. Her knuckles tighten
on the arm chair.

> AMY
> Hallie! Hallie! You understand
> nothing about Hallie! A self-centered,
> unpredictable girl - even to herself!
> (she regains control)
> Mister Linkhorn - my niece was
> bored that summer - visiting us in this
> dustbin of a town. You were an
> entertainment - a novelty ...

> EVA
> Amy! Don't be cruel! Please...

> AMY
> ...and she diverted herself with you!

For a moment Dove gazes at Amy. Then he speaks quietly,
but forcefully.

> DOVE
> Maybe it's you who can't understand
> her - or anything that's got to do
> with love. Livin' in this tomb, you....

> AMY
> (rising in anger)
> Get out!

Figure 12 (continued)

But Dove is carried away now. He pulls some letters out
of his pocket and rapidly, urgently, he opens one, seeking
out a paragraph to read. He finds what he's looking for.

>   DOVE
>   (desperately)
>   Listen - listen to this. It's from
>   Hallie... 'Sometimes when night
>   comes, it terrifies me and I cry
>   out, ''Where is Dove''? Dove and love!
>   The words go together - get mixed up.
>   Where is love? And I cry for that lost,
>   lovely summer...'

He stops reading, takes a moment to rein in his emotions.
Amy gazes at him grimly, intently. Finally:

>   AMY
>   Where is that from?

>   DOVE
>   New York. I got twelve letters
>   -- one every two, three days...

>   AMY
>   And then?

>   DOVE
>   Nothing! I've written twenty
>   times since then, and my
>   letters come back marked
>   'Address Unknown.'

>   EVA
>   Poor boy...

>   AMY
>   (cutting in harshly)
>   Obviously, my niece has lost interest
>   in you.

>   DOVE
>   No! That can't be. I only read you
>   part of the letter. Each one is more
>   needful of me than the one before.

Figure 12 (continued)

11a.

Amy watches him a moment - seems to soften.

                    AMY
          I'm sorry, Dove. But I can't tell you
          where she is.

                    DOVE
          You mean you're her only living
          relative and you don't know where
          she is?

                    AMY
               (hard again)
          I'm not used to being sassed in my
          own house, young man. I'll ask you
          to leave.

Dove hesitates, looking at her with pure hatred.

               AMY (cont.)
          What are you waiting for, the sheriff?

Abruptly, Dove turns and leaves. With a sudden, nervous
rapidity, Eva follows.

                Figure 12 (continued)

The next deletion following (2) eliminates Dove's attempt at self-defense, an attempt which weakens his position and his character. His ignoring of Amy's attack lends him dignity, and his persistence drives Amy into her brief outbreak, which tells us all we need to know at this point about her feelings toward her niece, and possibly a little about Hallie.

The deletion after (4) eliminates an unnecessarily cruel, and therefore unbelievable, reaction on Amy's part.

The cuts on page 10b are quite obvious. Dave's maudlin speeches are not only corny (since they come so early in the film that neither the story's basic situation nor Dove's character are yet established), they also tend to present him as a weak, unattractive person.

13   FULL SHOT   INT. GERARD SUNROOM   DAY

As Dove enters, the object that first pulls his eyes with
irresistible power is the painting over the fireplace.
The painting is impressionistic, unsparingly real -- a
face wreathed in some mysterious and indefinable pain.
Dove stares at it in confusion. Suddenly Eva breaks
the spell.

                          EVA
                It's a self-portrait.

                          DOVE   ①
                It -- it looks like Hallie --
                and yet it doesn't.

He turns toward Amy with an abrupt, pleading urgency.

                          DOVE (cont.)
                Miss Gerard, where is she?

                          AMY
                        (flatly)
                My condolences on the death of
                your father.

                          DOVE
                        (desperately)   OUT
                Where is Hallie, Ma'am?

                          AMY
                Her whereabouts are no business
                of yours.

                          EVA
                Amy...!

                          AMY
                        (ignoring her)
                My niece is not for you, Mister
                Linkhorn. Hallie was born and raised in   ②
                Europe -- in Paris. She's had everything
                -- known everything. Beside her, what
                are you? An uneducated dirt farmer.

                          DOVE
                        (fighting back)
                I'm through with farming. I   OUT
                mean to look into other things....

Figure 13

9b.

13   CONTINUED:

Amy makes a scoffing noise.

                    DOVE (cont.)
               Pa used to say no man can be   O UT
               sure of his callin' till he's
               thirty. That's when Christ
               got started.

                    AMY
          Sounds like Fitz Linkhorn, all right.

                    DOVE
                 (bursting out)   ③
          Tell me where Hallie is, Miss Gerard.

A flush of anger touches Amy's cheek. Her knuckles tighten
on the arm chair.

                    AMY
          Hallie! Hallie! You understand
          nothing about Hallie! A self-centered,   ④
          unpredictable girl - even to herself!
                 (she regains control)
          Mister Linkhorn - my niece was
          bored that summer - visiting us in
          this dustbin of a town. You were an
          entertainment - a novelty...

                    EVA   OUT
          Amy! Don't be cruel! Please...

                    AMY
          ...and she diverted herself with you!

For a moment Dove gazes at Amy. Then he speaks quietly,
but forcefully.

                    DOVE
          Maybe it's you who can't understand
          her - or anything that's got to do   ⑤
          with love. Livin' in this tomb, you....

                    AMY
                 (rising in anger)
          Get out!
                                                     CONT.

Figure 13 (continued)

10b.

13   CONTINUED:

But Dove is carried away now. He pulls some letters out
of his pocket and rapidly, urgently, he opens one, seeking
out a paragraph to read. He finds what he's looking for.

                    DOVE
                 (desperately)
        Listen - listen to this. It's from
        Hallie... 'Sometimes when night
        comes, it terrifies me and I cry
        out, ''Where is Dove''? Dove and love!
        The words go together - get mixed up.
        Where is love? And I cry for that lost,
        lovely summer...'

He stops reading, takes a moment to rein in his emotions.
Amy gazes at him grimly, intently. Finally:

                    AMY
        Where is that from?

                    DOVE
        New York. I got twelve letters
        -- one every two, three days...

                    AMY
        And then?

                    DOVE
        Nothing! I've written twenty
        times since then, and my
        letters come back marked
        'Address Unknown.'

                    EVA
        Poor boy...

                    AMY
                 (cutting in harshly)
        Obviously, my niece has lost interest
        in you.

                    DOVE
        No! That can't be. I only read you
        part of the letter. Each one is more
        needful of me than the one before.

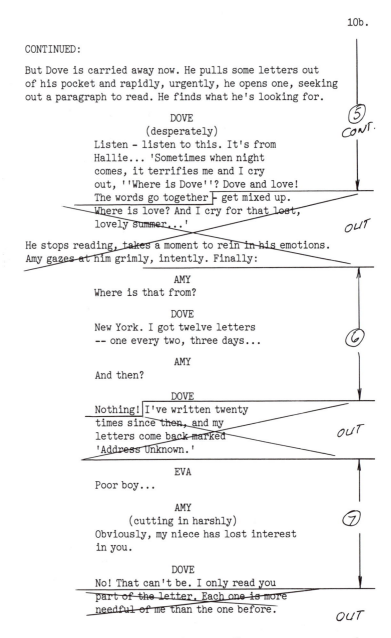

Figure 13 (continued)

13   CONTINUED:

Amy watches him a moment - seems to soften.

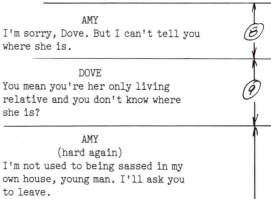

                        AMY
        I'm sorry, Dove. But I can't tell you
        where she is.

                        DOVE
        You mean you're her only living
        relative and you don't know where
        she is?

                        AMY
                    (hard again)
        I'm not used to being sassed in my
        own house, young man. I'll ask you
        to leave.

Dove hesitates, looking at her with pure hatred.

                    AMY (cont.)
        What are you waiting for, the sheriff?

Abruptly, Dove turns and leaves. With a sudden, nervous
rapidity, Eva follows.

Figure 13 (continued)

Figure 14 shows the scene as reedited, with the necessary
angles indicated. This kind of editing will not make a bad
scene great, but it can make it acceptable and useful. Since,
unfortunately, few films or film scripts are perfect, an editor
who can skillfully accomplish this kind of corrective manipulation will never lack a professional "home."

13   FULL SHOT   INT. GERARD SUNROOM   DAY

As Dove enters, the object that first pulls his eyes with
irresistible power is the painting over the fireplace.
The painting is impressionistic, unsparingly real -- a
face wreathed in some mysterious and indefinable pain.
Dove stares at it in confusion. Suddenly Eva breaks
the spell.

                         EVA
                It's a self-portrait.

                        DOVE
                It -- it looks like Hallie --
                and yet it doesn't.

He turns toward Amy with an abrupt, pleading urgency.

                    DOVE (cont.)
                Miss Gerard, where is she?

14   TWO SHOT   AMY AND EVA

                        AMY
                My niece is not for you, Mister
                Linkhorn. Hallie was born, and raised in
                Europe -- in Paris. She's had everything
                -- known everything. Beside her, what
                are you? An uneducated dirt farmer.

15   CLOSE SHOT   DOVE

He ignores the put-down.

                        DOVE
                Tell me where Hallie is, Miss Gerard.

16   CLOSE SHOT   AMY

                        AMY
                Hallie! Hallie! You understand
                nothing about Hallie! A self-centered,
                unpredictable girl - even to herself!

Figure 14

17   GROUP SHOT   DOVE, AMY, EVA

          For a moment Dove gazes at Amy. Then he speaks quietly,
          but forcefully.

                              DOVE
                    Maybe it's you who can't understand
                    her - or anything that's got to do
                    with love. Livin' in this tomb, you...

                              AMY
                         (rising in anger)
                    Get out!

          But Dove pulls some letters out of his pocket and opens
          one, seeking out a paragraph to read. He finds what he's
          looking for.

                              DOVE
                         (with some urgency)
                    Listen - listen to this. It's from
                    Hallie... 'Sometimes when night
                    comes it terrifies me and I cry
                    out, ''Where is Dove?'' Dove and love!
                    The words go together....

18   CLOSE SHOT   AMY

                              AMY
                         (cutting in)
                    Where is that from?

19   CLOSE SHOT   DOVE

                              DOVE
                    New York. I got twelve letters
                    -- one every two, three days...

                         AMY'S VOICE (O.S.)
                    and then?

                              DOVE
                    Nothing!

20   GROUP SHOT   DOVE, AMY, EVA

                              EVA
                    Poor boy...

                                        CONTINUED:

Figure 14 (continued)

10c.

20   CONTINUED:

                                AMY
                         (cutting in harshly)
               Obviously my niece has lost interest
               in you.

                              DOVE
               No! That can't be. I only...

21   CLOSE SHOT   AMY

                              AMY
                         (cutting in)
               I'm sorry, Dove. But I can't tell you
               where she is.

22   CLOSE SHOT   DOVE

                              DOVE
               You mean you're her only living
               relative and you don't know where
               she is?

23.   GROUP SHOT   AMY, DOVE, EVA

                              AMY
                         (hard again)
               I'm not used to being sassed in my
               own house, young man. I'll ask you
               to leave.

     Dove hesitates, looking at her with hatred.

                        AMY (cont.)
               What are you waiting for, the sheriff?

     Abruptly, Dove turns and leaves. With a sudden, nervous
     rapidity, Eva follows.

                 Figure 14 (continued)

Our third example is another scene from *The Carpetbaggers*. It is neither a bad nor an inadequate scene—in truth, Bob Cummings and Marty Balsam, two exceptional actors, played it extremely well. It is used here only to show what kind of manipulation is possible if such a scene should require shortening, and how new elements, not originally planned or shot, can be inserted.

Figure 15 is the scene in a master shot, as written.

146   INT. NORMAN'S LIVING ROOM   CLOSE SHOT   NORMAN   NIGHT

Norman, rumpled from sleep is in his pyjamas, robe,
slippers. There is a shocked look on his face as he stares
at someone O.S.

                    NORMAN
              She's not dead?

147   TWO SHOT   NORMAN AND PIERCE

Dan Pierce, in sport coat, and sport shirt open at the
throat, is standing across from Norman. There are only
a couple of lights on in the room. Pierce is agitated,
nervous.

                    PIERCE
              Not quite. She's unconscious.
              But the doctor didn't give much for
              her chances of coming out of it.

                    NORMAN
              Have you told Jonas?

                    PIERCE
              I'm afraid to. That's why I came
              here first. I'm trying to work my
              way up to him.

Norman bangs his hand down on the coffee table, gets up
and starts pacing.

                    NORMAN
              How could she do this to me! Cord wants
              this studio more than anything in the
              world. Once he finds out about Rina, I
              haven't a prayer of selling.

                    PIERCE
              You know, I never realized what
              a cold-blooded character you are.

                    NORMAN
              This is a one star studio. If she goes,
              we go. Can I keep her alive? I got to
              think of the living - and that's me.
                    (Pierce snorts)
              You, too! Your job dies with Rina!

                    Figure 15

147   CONTINUED:

                              PIERCE
              Yeah -
                    (then more concerned)
              I never thought of that.

                             NORMAN
                  (a nasty laugh)
              You get cold-blooded fast yourself,
              don't you?

                             PIERCE
              You just shot me with an icicle!

                           NORMAN
                  (dropping the bait)
              Of course, you could fix it so you
              wouldn't have to worry about working.
              Ever.

                           PIERCE
              I don't follow ....

                           NORMAN
                You're sure Jonas doesn't know
              about the accident yet?

                           PIERCE
              I'm sure.

Norman suddenly turns away.

                           NORMAN
              No, it wouldn't work. He'll hear
              about - the papers - the radio...

                           PIERCE
              It happened too late for the morning
              papers, and he never listens to the
              radio...

                           NORMAN
              The reporters....

                           PIERCE
              He never answers the phone at night.

Norman faces Pierce.

                           NORMAN
              You think you could keep Cord from
              learning about the accident for a few
              hours?

Figure 15 (continued)

147   CONTINUED:

                              PIERCE
                    Oh, now...wait a minute...

                              NORMAN
                    How much was he willing to pay to buy
                    me out?

                              PIERCE
                    Oh - three or four million.

                              NORMAN
                    I'll start at five. And if the deal comes
                    off you get fifteen percent.

                              PIERCE
                             (stunned)
                    Fif - fifteen percent?

                              NORMAN
                    It's worth it.

          Pierce has to sit down. Norman continues his attack.

                              NORMAN
                    I've waited a long time for a chance
                    like this!

                              PIERCE
                             (uncertainly)
                    But - but suppose he finds out - I mean
                    about me setting him up for the kill?
                    I'm taking a terrible chance.

                              NORMAN
                    It'll be worth every penny. And at least
                    this way you come out with something.
                    With no Rina - and no studio - how long
                    do you think he'll wait to fire you? So
                    get busy.

                              PIERCE
                    Suppose he won't meet this morning?

                              NORMAN
                    See that he does - for fifteen percent
                    of five million!

                    Figure 15 (continued)

147   CONTINUED:

                              PIERCE
                            (sweating)
                    That's -- that's seven hundred and
                    fifty thousand dollars!

                              NORMAN
                    Quite a nest egg!

                              PIERCE
                    Yeah!

Norman pulls Pierce up out of the chair.

                              NORMAN
                    So get going. I'll pull my lawyers out
                    of bed and have them draw up two letters
                    of agreement. We'll sign yours first.

                              PIERCE
                    Yeah - sure.

Norman propels Pierce toward the door.

                              NORMAN
                    This is the day we pluck Jonas Cord's
                    feathers! Eight o'clock at his hotel.
                            (he opens the door)
                    Don't be a minute late.

                              PIERCE
                    No, no, of course not. Not a minute
                    late.

He goes out the door in a daze. Norman is keen for the
battle.

                                              DISSOLVE TO:

                    Figure 15 (continued)

Figure 16 indicates the deletions, which total about three-fourths of a page, and the sequence of cuts in a new alignment.

137b.

146   INT. NORMAN'S LIVING ROOM   CLOSE SHOT   NORMAN   NIGHT

         Norman, rumpled from sleep is in his pyjamas, robe,
         slippers. There is a shocked look on his face as he stares
         at someone O.S.

                              NORMAN
                    She's not dead?

147   TWO SHOT   NORMAN AND PIERCE

         Dan Pierce, in sport coat, and sport shirt open at the
         throat, is standing across from Norman. There are only
         a couple of lights on in the room. Pierce is agitated,
         nervous.

                              PIERCE
                    Not quite. She's unconscious.
                    But the doctor didn't give much for
                    her chances of coming out of it.

                              NORMAN
                    Have you told Jonas?

                              PIERCE
                    I'm afraid to. That's why I came
                    here first. I'm trying to work my
                    way up to him.

         Norman bangs his hand down on the coffee table, gets up
         and starts pacing.

                              NORMAN
                    How could she do this to me! Cord wants
                    this studio more than anything in the
                    world. Once he finds out about Rina, I
                    haven't a prayer of selling.

                              PIERCE
                    You know, I never realized what
                    a cold-blooded character you are.

                              NORMAN
                    This is a one star studio. If she goes,   OUT
                    we go. Can I keep her alive? I got to
                    think of the living - and that's me.
                         (Pierce snorts)
                    You, too! Your job dies with Rina!

                              Figure 16

138b.

147   CONTINUED: (3)

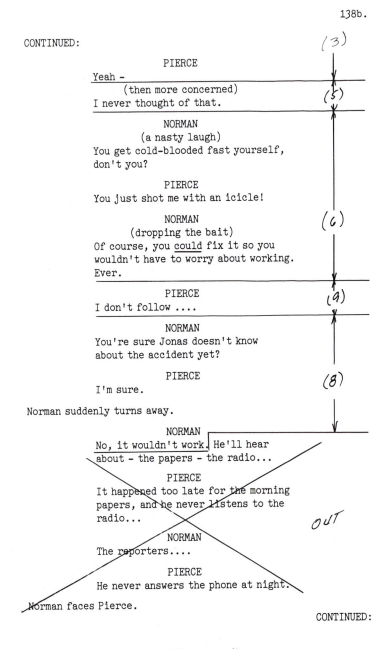

                              PIERCE
                   Yeah -
                         (then more concerned)   (5)
                   I never thought of that.

                              NORMAN
                           (a nasty laugh)
                   You get cold-blooded fast yourself,
                   don't you?

                              PIERCE
                   You just shot me with an icicle!

                              NORMAN
                           (dropping the bait)   (6)
                   Of course, you could fix it so you
                   wouldn't have to worry about working.
                   Ever.

                              PIERCE
                   I don't follow ....   (9)

                              NORMAN
                   You're sure Jonas doesn't know
                   about the accident yet?

                              PIERCE
                   I'm sure.   (8)

            Norman suddenly turns away.

                              NORMAN
                   No, it wouldn't work. He'll hear
                   about - the papers - the radio...

                              PIERCE
                   It happened too late for the morning
                   papers, and he never listens to the
                   radio...   OUT

                              NORMAN
                   The reporters....

                              PIERCE
                   He never answers the phone at night.

            Norman faces Pierce.

                                                    CONTINUED:

                   Figure 16 (continued)

139b.

147   CONTINUED:

                              NORMAN
                 You think you could keep Cord from   (1 2)
                 learning about the accident for a few
                 hours?

                              PIERCE   (1 3)
                 Oh, now...wait a minute...

                              NORMAN   (1 0)
                 How much was he willing to pay to buy
                 me out?

                              PIERCE   (1 1)
                 Oh - three or four million.

                              NORMAN
                 I'll start at five. And if the deal comes
                 off you get fifteen percent.

                              PIERCE
                              (stunned)
                 Fif - fifteen percent?

                              NORMAN
                 It's worth it.
                                                             (1 4)
        Pierce has to sit down. Norman continues his attack.

                              NORMAN
                 I've waited a long time for a chance
                 like this!

                              PIERCE
                              (uncertainly)
                 But - suppose he finds out - I mean
                 about me setting him up for the kill?
                 I'm taking a terrible chance.

                              NORMAN
                 It'll be worth every penny. And at least
                 this way you come out with something.   OUT
                 With no Rina - and no studio - how long
                 do you think he'll wait to fire you? So
                 get busy.

                        Figure 16 (continued)

140b.

147   CONTINUED: OUT

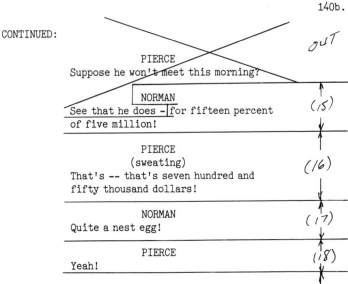

                    PIERCE
     Suppose he won't meet this morning?

                    NORMAN   (15)
     See that he does - for fifteen percent
     of five million!

                    PIERCE
                   (sweating)   (16)
     That's -- that's seven hundred and
     fifty thousand dollars!

                    NORMAN   (17)
     Quite a nest egg!

                    PIERCE   (18)
     Yeah!

Norman pulls Pierce up out of the chair.

                    NORMAN
     So get going. I'll pull my lawyers out
     of bed and have them draw up two letters
     of agreement. We'll sign yours first.

                    PIERCE
     Yeah - sure.   (19)

Norman propels Pierce toward the door.

                    NORMAN
     This is the day we pluck Jonas Cord's
     feathers! Eight o'clock at his hotel.
               (he opens the door)
     Don't be a minute late.

                    PIERCE
     No, no, of course not. Not a minute
     late.

He goes out the door in a daze. Norman is keen for the
battle.

                                          DISSOLVE TO:

                    Figure 16 (continued)

Now, the analysis: The first deletion, after cut (1), is made to get a more spontaneous, emotional response to Pierce's accusation. Cuts (2), (3), (4), and (5), which follow, are rearranged and played in close shots to continue this more realistic and more understandable self-justification by Norman. It also accentuates Pierce's awakening to his own tenuous situation.

The next three lines follow in original order, but then a cut is inserted (scene 153, page 138c in Figure 17) that was not in the original scene, nor was such a cut shot. But it is easily manufactured by finding a suitable reaction from one of Pierce's close-ups, even if an "out take" has to be printed. The sound "Hm?" is "looped" in during postproduction without any additional effort or expense since a certain amount of looping for various scenes in the film is almost always required.

The cut is inserted at this point in the scene to show Pierce beginning to catch on to Norman's ploy somewhat earlier than in the original scene. It also reminds the viewer of Pierce's "conman" attributes.

Cut (9) is reserved for a moment as (8) follows the manufactured close shot (153). Now (9) drops into place, primarily to keep Norman rolling. Cuts (10) (11) (12) and (13) are rearranged to permit a slightly more subtle approach from Norman. Cut (14) now continues as in the original lineup, with the hook being set. Only one more tug at the line is needed here, and it is most effectively furnished by an appeal to Pierce's greed through the direct reference "for fifteen percent of five million!" Considering the characters involved, this attack is much more effective than reiteration of the threat to Pierce's job. New jobs are not that hard to find, but $750,000 is!

Although no picture cut is made, a new element is inserted into (14)—the "Yeah" in scene 160, page 140c. It serves to separate Norman's non-sequitor lines, "It's worth it" and "I've waited (etc.)" and to strengthen Pierce's decision just before his final doubt. The "Yeah," really a loud breath, is stolen from the sound track of one of his takes or looped later if a satisfactory reading cannot be found. It is inserted just when Pierce sits down, which will help to distract the viewer's attention from his lips. The sound, in fact, requires no lip movement, and its inclusion will by no means appear to be obvious. This kind of "manufacturing" can be accomplished easily, even on a much more complex level, and it should always be kept in mind as a possible lifebelt in severely troubled, sink-or-swim situations.

The rest of the scene runs as written, except that cuts (15), (16), (17), and (18) are played in close shots to allow for neater timing and closer interplay.

146   CLOSE SHOT   NORMAN'S LIVING ROOM NORMAN NIGHT

Norman, rumpled from sleep is in his pyjamas, robe,
slippers. There is a shocked look on his face as he stares
at someone O.S.

                         NORMAN
              She's not dead?

147   TWO SHOT   NORMAN AND PIERCE

Dan Pierce, in sport coat, and sport shirt open at the
throat, is standing across from Norman. There are only
a couple of lights on in the room. Pierce is agitated,
nervous.

                         PIERCE
              Not quite. She's unconscious.
              But the doctor didn't give much for
              her chances of coming out of it.

                         NORMAN
              Have you told Jonas?

                         PIERCE
              I'm afraid to. That's why I came
              here first. I'm trying to work my
              way up to him.

Norman bangs his hand down on the coffee table, gets up
and starts pacing.

                         NORMAN
              How could she do this to me! Cord wants
              this studio more than anything in the
              world. Once he finds out about Rina, I
              haven't a prayer of selling.

                         PIERCE
              You know, I never realized what
              a cold-blooded character you are.

148   CLOSE SHOT   NORMAN

                         NORMAN
              Can I keep her alive? I got to
              think of the living - and that's me.

                         Figure 17

138c.

149   CLOSE SHOT   PIERCE

                                        PIERCE
                              Yeah...

150   CLOSE SHOT   NORMAN

                                        NORMAN
                              You, too! Your job dies with Rina!

151   CLOSE SHOT   PIERCE

           Suddenly concerned.

                                        PIERCE
                              I never thought of that.

152   TWO SHOT   NORMAN AND PIERCE

                                        NORMAN
                              You get cold-blooded fast yourself,
                              don't you?

                                        PIERCE
                              You just shot me with an icicle!

                                        NORMAN
                                    (dropping the bait)
                              Of course, you <u>could</u> fix it so you
                              wouldn't have to worry about working.
                              Ever.

153   CLOSE SHOT   PIERCE

                                        PIERCE
                                    (suddenly alert)
                              Hm?

154   CLOSE SHOT   NORMAN

                                        NORMAN
                              You're sure Jonas doesn't know about
                              the accident yet.

                                    PIERCE'S VOICE (O.S.)
                              I'm sure.

           Norman suddenly turns away.

                                                              CONTINUED:

                              Figure 17 (continued)

154   CONTINUED:

                           NORMAN
                    No, it wouldn't work.

155   CLOSE SHOT   PIERCE

                           PIERCE
                    I don't follow....

156   CLOSE SHOT   NORMAN

                           NORMAN
                    How much was he willing to pay to buy
                    me out.

157   CLOSE SHOT   PIERCE

                           PIERCE
                    Oh - three or four million.

158   CLOSE SHOT   NORMAN

                           NORMAN
                    You think you could keep Cord from learning
                    about the accident for a few hours?

159   CLOSE SHOT   PIERCE

                           PIERCE
                    Oh, now...wait a minute....

160   TWO SHOT   NORMAN AND PIERCE

                           NORMAN
                    I'll start at five. And if the deal comes
                    off you get fifteen percent.

                           PIERCE
                          (stunned)
                    Fif - fifteen percent?

                           NORMAN
                    It's worth it.

                    Figure 17 (continued)

160   CONTINUED:

                            PIERCE
                        (as he sits down)
                Yeah...

                            NORMAN
                        (continues his attack)
                I've waited a long time for a chance
                like this!

                            PIERCE
                        (uncertainly)
                But - but suppose he finds out - I mean
                about me setting him up for the kill?
                I'm taking a terrible chance.

161   CLOSE SHOT   NORMAN

                            NORMAN
                For fifteen percent of five million.

162   CLOSE SHOT   PIERCE

                            PIERCE
                        (sweating)
                That's - that's seven hundred and
                fifty thousand dollars!

163   CLOSE SHOT   NORMAN

                            NORMAN
                Quite a nest egg!

164   CLOSE SHOT   PIERCE

                            PIERCE
                Yeah!

165   TWO SHOT   PIERCE AND NORMAN

         Norman pulls Pierce up out of the chair.

                            NORMAN
                So get going. I'll pull my lawyers out
                of bed and have them draw up two letters
                of agreement. We'll sign yours first.

                        Figure 17 (continued)

165   CONTINUED:

                         PIERCE
                  Yeah - sure.

Norman propels Pierce toward the door.

                         NORMAN
                  This is the day we pluck Jonas Cord's
                  feathers! Eight o'clock at his hotel.
                       (he opens the door)
                  Don't be a minute late.

                         PIERCE
                  No, no, of course not. Not a minute
                  late.

He goes out the door in a daze. Norman is keen for the
battle.

                                            DISSOLVE TO:

                  Figure 17 (continued)

16

Rescuing the Actor

One more important area remains to be discussed—selective editing of inadequate acting. I am not talking about *bad* acting; the only ameliorative measure an editor can take in such a circumstance is to diminish the misery as much as possible. I am talking about acting which, for one reason or another, fails to hit the mark.

The best example of corrective treatment of such acting is one I have referred to on previous occasions. It is a prime example of serendipity rather than of creative ability; the result of an effort to make the best of a difficult situation rather than a rationally conceived and executed editing accomplishment. With the publisher's permission, I shall borrow the episode from my book, *On Film Directing.* *

> *Ruggles of Red Gap*, directed by Leo McCarey, starred Charles Laughton and Charlie Ruggles. Laughton had a "rubber" face and, although certainly a fine actor, was occasionally guilty of severe attacks of "mugging," especially in moments of high emotional involvement. I was forced to cut around, or away from, much of his face-making, but one sequence presented a nearly impossible problem. The scene was set in a western saloon. Laughton, playing Charlie Ruggles' very

*Dmytryk, E., *On Film Directing*, Boston, Focal Press, 1983.

English butler (won in a poker game from a British lord), has accom-
panied his new boss to the bar. At one point Ruggles wishes to quote
from Lincoln's Gettysburg Address, but can't remember the speech.
Neither can any other member of his party, nor any of the saloon's
habitues.

Suddenly, Ruggles attention is arrested by Laughton, who is mur-
muring, "Four score and seven years ago. . . ." Amazed to learn that
the Englishman knows the words, Ruggles encourages him to continue.

Laughton was highly emotional and extremely nervous. Filming his
shot alone, in medium close-up, occupied a day and a half. McCarey
patiently shot the scene from 40 to 50 times, rarely getting a complete
take, and never a perfect one. Finally Laughton, with tears streaming
from his eyes, dropped to his knees and begged for mercy. McCarey
decided to postpone further shooting.

At this point I suggested that it might be possible to patch together
a complete sound track by using the best parts of a number of takes.
McCarey agreed. To begin with, I worked only with the sound track,
checking out all the 15 or 20 printed takes and an even greater number
of "outs." Using a line here, a phrase there, sometimes only a word or
two, I pieced together a complete version of the speech. McCarey listened to it, liked what he heard, and asked me to complete it.

So far my efforts had been little more than routine. Now came the
hard part. Fitting the picture to the track brought chaos, since each of
the sound cuts needed a matching picture. Only one solution presented itself. The speech was started in a setup over Laughton's back,
followed by cuts of the reactions of others in the saloon—first, Charlie
Ruggles and his table companions, and then other onlookers as, one by
one, they left their stools and walked over for a closer look and listen.
Offscreen, the butler's voice grew in strength as he gained confidence,
and the speech ended triumphantly to the barkeeper's "Drinks on the
house."

Dramatic logic holds that at least a large part of the speech should
have been played on the scene's central character, the butler. But every
matching cut of Laughton showed his rather generous lips blubbering,
his eyes turning upward in their sockets, and huge tears rolling down
his cheeks. So, except for two short cuts, the entire speech was played
over shots of the onlookers.

At the executive running, Ernst Lubitsch, then head of Paramount
production, suggested that since the scene belonged to Laughton, we
should see more of him. McCarey agreed, and I was outvoted. I
selected a pair of the most innocuous cuts and added them for the
sneak preview.

Ruggles of Red Gap turned out to be one of that year's top films. At
the preview, it played beautifully—up to the Gettysburg Address. The
scene started, the players reacted, everything went well. Then came
the first cut of Laughton, tears streaming down his cheeks as he spoke.
Americans admire the Gettysburg Address, but they don't cry over it.

The audience burst into laughter, which continued to build throughout the rest of the now inaudible speech. But laughter, at the expense of Lincoln's noble phrases, was not what we were looking for. One of the film's key scenes had been torpedoed.

As we left the theater after the preview, McCarey said, "Put it back the way you had it." I did, and the next preview confirmed our original judgment. This time there was no laughter. The audience listened attentively and applauded Laughton's performance. From that day until the end of Laughton's life, hardly a Lincoln's birthday passed without one of the major radio networks inviting him to once again deliver the Gettysburg Address.

This example illustrates not only the part luck can play in the editorial construction of an important sequence, but it also focuses attention on what may be the most difficult, perhaps (in my opinion at least) most creative, and potentially useful editing technique of the future—the old art of montage.

17

Where It All Began— The Montage

There are two basic types of montage. What is sometimes referred to as the *Hollywood montage* differs substantially from the *European montage*. The latter, developed to its highest level by the Russian filmmakers of the 1920s, used a carefully designed and edited series of straight cuts to develop story, situation, and character; it is most effectively demonstrated in the celebrated "Odessa steps" sequence in Eisenstein's *Battleship Potemkin*.

The Hollywood montage, on the other hand, is almost invariably a transition. It too is composed of a number of silent cuts, often in a series of dissolves, and always musically underscored, but there its similarity to its foreign cousin ends. It is, in truth, simply a more complicated, and often more pretentious, version of the straight dissolve.

A familiar example: As a sequence ends, the camera dollys in to a shot of a window. Through it we see a tree in full summer foliage. Now the scene dissolves to another shot of the same window (often an exact duplicate of the preceding set-up), but the tree is now bare. The next shot shows the tree and the surrounding terrain covered by a blanket of snow. The final dissolve discloses the tree heavily loaded with blossoms, and as the camera pulls back to a full shot of the interior of the room and a new scene gets under way, the viewer knows that approximately 1 year has elapsed.

A similar series is often used to convey transition in space. A shot of New York's skyline dissolves to the cornfields of the Middle West, then to a spectacular shot of the Rocky Mountains, and finally to a shot of the Golden Gate Bridge, taking us pictorially across the breadth of the United States. It may not be as economical as a shot of a character saying "I'm flying to San Francisco," but it's a lot prettier, and when constructed in less hackneyed style, it is better storytelling. (Obviously, the preceding time transition montage would not work for "Hawaii Five-O," nor would a location transition connecting less well known places have any meaning. Problem: How would one devise a seasonal transition for a tropical location or a location transition transporting the viewer from Riyadh to Timbuktu?)

The Hollywood montage is also used as a means of exposing a character's unspoken thoughts or to pictorialize his sub-conscious experiences, as in dreams or nightmares. Such montages are really moving collages, and their effectiveness depends in great part on the creativeness and dramatic skill of the editor.

Much ingenuity has been expended in countless efforts at originality, but the weight of past accomplishments makes such efforts increasingly difficult to realize. In many instances, the efforts are abandoned, and the desired objectives are achieved through a simple exchange of dialogue or, in a sometimes desperate throwback to earlier times, by the use of titles. But each new film presents new opportunities, and in the words of the old pro, "Whatever the technique—if it does the job, use it."

It is unfortunately true that many screenwriters, especially those schooled in television, still think in terms of dialogue when constructing a transition in time or place, but the recent experiments with old techniques seem to indicate that the viewer would rather see it than hear it. Expository dialogue is still anathema to any filmmaker with talent or taste, and a good editor with a bent for resourcefulness and an eye for imagery can please the viewer's visual sense, develop the situation, and still save time by creating a pictorial transition.

Even in Hollywood films, the opportunity to build a montage that carries the developmental potential of a regular sequence does occasionally present itself. Such opportunities arise most frequently in suspense films, and an effective one is found in *Murder, My Sweet*, the 1944 version of Raymond Chandler's, *Farewell, My Lovely*.

At one point in the film, Phillip Marlowe, played by Dick Powell, is laid low by the usual blow to the head. A recurring effect, an engulfing black cloud, wipes out the scene. It clears up to show a somewhat distorted shot of Marlowe being dumped into an elevator. The next cut shows him regaining consciousness just as the elevator tips forward to send him sliding through the open door. Now the camera falls with him as he flails away at empty space while the isolated elevator car accelerates off into an abysmal background. Next, Marlowe laboriously climbs a steep flight of stairs, only to be confronted by the gigantic, menacing faces of his tormentors. Whether drugged or frightened into a panic, he grabs for the stair railing, only to have it melt under his hand. Once more he falls headlong into a black, bottomless pit. Now Marlowe approaches a series of doors—doorframes, really—set out in empty space. As he stumbles through them, leisurely pursued by a man in a white laboratory coat, each succeeding door is progressively smaller until, as he reaches the end of the line, he can barely squeeze his head through the opening. (This effect was borrowed from one of my own recurring nightmares.)

The man in the white coat, seen for the first time in the film, has kept pace with Marlowe by walking through the doors as if they weren't there. He carries a syringe. As Marlowe thrusts his head through the last tiny doorframe, he looks up to see the cruel, sardonic face of his pursuer. Marlowe raises his hand in a feeble gesture of defiance, and we cut to a close insert of a giant-sized syringe as it plunges toward the camera. Marlowe falls away once more, and the whole picture goes into a rapid spin, which, as it slows to a stop, turns out to be a ceiling fixture seen through a tattered screen of smoke. The camera pulls back to disclose Marlowe lying on a small bed in a sparsely furnished room. Although the smoke effect continues to diffuse the scene, we know we are now looking at reality as seen through Marlowe's drug-bemused eyes.

For the technically minded, here is a breakdown of the montage. It starts from the center of the black-out effect.

		Time (in seconds)	Total time (in seconds)
1.	Marlowe is dragged into elevator	10.0	
2.	Marlow regains consciousness, slides out of elevator	5.8	15.8
3.	Marlowe falls away from elevator	4.2	20.0
4.	Medium shot of Marlowe climbing stairs toward camera; large heads of Moose and Marriot appear in background	4.3	24.3
5.	Close over-shoulder shot of Marlowe; in background large close-up of Marriot dissolves into a large close-up of Moose; Moose reaches out for Marlowe	4.4	28.7
6.	Close-up of Marlowe, reacts to vision	1.1	29.8
7.	Over-shoulder shot of Marlowe; close-up of Moose in background (a continuation of shot 5)	1.0	30.8
8.	Medium shot of Marlowe leaning back on melting handrail; he falls	3.8	34.6
9.	Marlowe falls through space	6.6	41.2
	A wavering dissolve to:		
10.	Long shot of line of doors; Marlowe enters shot, stops at first door, looks back over his shoulder	4.2	45.4
	(With this shot a superimposition begins—a ragged cobweb effect—which continues over all shots to the end of the montage.)		
11.	Close-up of Moose; dissolves to close-up of man in a white laboratory coat	2.6	48.0
12.	Close-up of Marlowe; reacts and starts through the first door	2.0	50.0
13.	Full shot from behind Marlowe as he goes through the first door; man in white follows through closed door	9.5	59.5

		Time (in seconds)	Total time (in seconds)
14.	Front medium shot of Marlowe through second door (in foreground); man in white follows	4.0	63.5
15.	Close over-shoulder shot as Marlowe reaches last door and looks back at pursuer	2.2	65.7
16.	Close-up of man in white as he walks toward Marlowe	1.1	66.8
17.	Over-shoulder close-up of Marlowe as he starts through last door	1.2	68.0
18.	Close-up of Marlowe as he comes through door toward camera and sees:	1.4	69.4
19.	Close-up of man in white confronting him	1.4	70.8
20.	Insert syringe	2.0	72.8
21.	Marlowe falls back through door	0.7	73.5
22.	Marlowe falls through spinning hole	6.5	80.0
	Dissolve to:		
23.	Spinning ceiling light; when it stops, the cobweb effect has subtly changed to a moderately heavy frozen smoke effect; to stop of spinning	6.5	86.5

Note: In general, the cuts become shorter as the montage builds to a climax.

This series of dissolves and straight cuts lasts less than a minute and a half, but in that short time we are able to cover a passage of days, to introduce a new face (that of the spurious psychiatrist, whose character and purpose are immediately clear), and to develop a new plot situation—all without resorting to a single line of expository dialogue.

This montage was originally intended to be a concoction of surrealistic scenes, in the style of Salvador Dali, but at the last moment it was decided to use more translatable imagery. Dramatizing the commonly experienced dream sensations of falling, spinning, and claustrophobic spaces encourages the viewer to identify with Marlowe's state of mind, and avoiding the explicit encourages him to share Marlowe's bewilderment, to live with him through his moments of terror, rather than to regard them from a distance with a clinical eye.

The building of such a pictorial sequence, with its sense of personal creative involvement, evokes some of the feeling of the early "story-on-the-back-of-a-menu" days and affords the editor a very special pleasure. It is the nearest thing we have to that triumph of ingenuity over ignorance, the "creative editing" of Kuleshov, Eisenstein, Pudovkin, and others.

In the first quarter of this century, the screen was dumb. Since 90 percent of the Russian people were illiterate, titles were useless. There was, of course, an alternative, but pantomime, although a fine art, is the antithesis of screen acting, which must present at least the appearance of reality. Working within this limitation, the Russian filmmakers were occasionally able to construct amazingly real films by creating montages of carefully shot and cleverly juxtaposed images. Their techniques have been fully described and analyzed by the creators and practitioners of the art and by many of their admirers. Here I will offer only an example or two and draw some conclusions as to their possible value for modern films.

Example 1: In an oversimplification typical of early films, Eisenstein's *The Old and the New* (*The General Line*) shows an instructor demonstrating the use of a mechanical cream separator to a skeptical audience of backward peasants.* The success or failure of the instructor's demonstration will determine his success or failure in organizing a collective.

The ragged peasants, some 20 or 30 in all, are assembled in a bare room, staring at a covered object some 5 feet in height. A number of group shots and close-ups of the doubting Thomases, interspersed with cuts of the somewhat anxious instructor, create anticipatory suspense. Then, with the flourish of a magician disclosing a mysteriously manifested cage of white doves, the instructor uncovers the separator.

In an unusual sequence of cuts, the act of flipping off the machine's covering is played in two separate and different setups. The movement at the beginning of the second cut actually overlaps, or repeats, the movement of the last half of the first cut. In the continuation of the action, the drape's landing on the floor is played in three separate and similarly overlapping cuts.

---

*Few students today will know what a cream separator is. It need only be known that it separates whole milk into two of its components—cream and skim milk. Centrifugal force is the operating principle, and each of the milk components issues out of its own separate spout.

This series of cuts creates an interesting effect—it gives an "entrance" to an inanimate object. Drawing out the action of the removal, the tossing aside, and the landing of the drape supplies the climax dramatically demanded by the suspense which leads up to the separator's introduction. It also lends greater emphasis to the subsequent scenes.

For now a new suspense buildup begins. The instructor laboriously starts to crank the heavy flywheel which, through a chain of gears, spins the milk-containing chamber. When it has acquired a bit of momentum, he turns the job over to a young, obviously eager peasant. A long series of cuts follows, with the action roughly divided into three parts. First, close-ups and group shots of the peasants intercut with shots of the revolving flywheel, spinning gears, and whirling milk establish and build the peasants' growing disdain as cuts to the spouts show no results. Interestingly, in this section only the machine moves—the reactions of the humans are fixed in still shots, each one a portrait worthy of a gallery showing. The symbolism of the static peasants opposed to the dynamism of the machine is obvious but effective.

But soon the watchers' aloof skepticism turns to laughter and sneers. The reactions of the instructor and his two peasant supporters show increasing anxiety. As their frustration deepens, movement number two begins. A cut of one of the nozzles shows what might be a pulsating drop of white liquid just beginning to form. Now the shots of the instructor and the peasants mirror the expected changes in attitudes as further cuts to the machine disclose that the skim milk and the cream are indeed beginning to ooze out of their respective spouts. These cuts build slowly—several cuts of the spouts are needed to convince the peasants (and us) that the white liquid is really starting to flow.

The third development is triumphant. The machine pours out streams of skim milk and cream. The instructor, his young helper, and the peasant woman who has been the prime mover in the demonstration are ecstatic; the peasants are now all firm believers. A few gratuitous shots of leaping fountains of water dissolve us through to the next sequence, which shows milk cows being delivered to the now organized collective, naturally.

This sequence is some 6 minutes in length, and in the 6 minutes, the viewer is completely convinced that the once skeptical peasants are ready to give up their ''old'' practices of manual labor for the ''new''—the mechanization of their daily work.

A montage of this sort is truly a realization of the old adage ''One picture is worth a thousand words.'' A successful demonstration is always more convincing than a verbal argument, as any good salesman knows. Obviously, few people today are interested in cream separators, but the principles involved in the sequence have wide application. Every dramatic structure or movement depends on change—change of attitude, of action, or of direction—and these changes must be found understandable and acceptable by the viewer, who cannot be conditioned as arbitrarily as a character in a script.

Let us create another example of the power of an image to clarify a subtle thought or idea—this one from the world of science. Most people are aware that matter is supposed to consist of submicroscopic particles whirling at great speed in relatively vast areas of space. Yet it is very difficult to convince a person that the hardwood coffee table on which he props his feet is almost complete emptiness. He will hear your words, but his senses will call you a liar. So let us develop a series of images, of cuts.

First, a stationary bicycle wheel. Its spokes, although clearly visible, occupy only a small percentage of the space between the hub and the rim. Even a blind person can easily poke a finger through any number of places without fear of damage. Now spin the wheel rapidly. The spokes disappear, showing a slightly diffused area between rim and hub which seems quite empty. Yet even a person with 20/20 vision would not dare try to push a finger through that apparently empty space—it is as solid as a board and twice as dangerous. This exercise is an oversimplification, but properly presented, it can help a viewer understand how apparently empty space can become rockhard when rapid movement is involved.

The foregoing example is somewhat abstruse and removed, but so are many problems of human interrelations, which are the building blocks of drama. Just as a free, rapidly deflating toy balloon can tell you more about jet propulsion than most textbooks, so Hitchcock's murder-in-the-shower-bath montage (in *Psycho*) is far more vivid and immediate than any verbal or normal pictorial rendering could possibly be. If clever cutting can make a star out of a cream separator or furnish a useful explanation of atomic movement, think of what could be done with a scene in which the central figures were Paul Newman and. . . .

Which brings us back to the present and a vividly dramatized scene in *The Verdict*. It is quite short, and it is not a true montage, but it approaches that technique in its creative use of the image as a substitute for dialogue.

Newman must find a particular nurse to testify for him in a "wrongful death" trial. Her testimony is of vital importance—his case, his reputation, and his future as a lawyer all depend on it. Yet the nurse is so frightened for her own safety that she has left town and changed her name and her job to avoid any involvement in the proceedings. Obviously, obtaining her cooperation will be difficult—probably impossible.

Newman finally locates her, but in order to see her he is forced to disguise his purpose, his profession, and even his place of residence. His deceptive approach has barely begun when she sees, carelessly exposed in his breast pocket, the shuttle flight envelope which shows he has come from Boston, the scene of the crime.

In a close-up, she looks at him, traumatized, her eyes showing her fear and her awareness of his true mission. In his close-up, in turn, he pleads silently. Back to her—her eyes fill with tears as she begins to cry quietly. Now Newman speaks, "Will you help me?" And the sequence ends. We know that she will cooperate, whatever the consequences, although not a single word relating to the true purpose of the confrontation has been uttered.

It is great acting, but it is also a brilliant series of cuts, an example of "movies" at their best. No playwright, past or present, could, with dialogue, have presented a scene half as concise, and no other theatrical medium could even have begun to duplicate its effectiveness. It is a rare example of the aborted art of montage, an oasis in the desert. And if, to quote Lindgren once more, "the development of film technique has been primarily the development of editing," and I believe it has, then a reinvestigation of the art of "creative editing" is the only way to reach the green fields beyond.

Epilogue

Rule 7: Substance first—then form.

Norman Cousins, in one of his perceptive editorials, wrote, "We are turning out young men and women who are superbly trained but poorly educated. They are a how-to generation, less concerned with the nature of things than with the working of things. They are beautifully skilled but intellectually underdeveloped. They know everything that is to be known about the functional requirements of their trade but very little about the *human situation* that serves as the context for their work."* (italics added).

Six years of teaching have made me acutely aware of the truth of Mr. Cousins' words. They have also convinced me that the condition he describes derives not only from the students' desires, but also from the teachers' aims. Which leads me, at the risk of being charged with redundancy, to offer a few final words of advice: This book has persistently stressed technique and has urged the pursuit of perfection in its use. But the "human situation," in all its guises, is what good films are all about, and technical skill counts for nothing if it is used only to manufacture films which have little to do with humanity.

*From *Saturday Review*, May-June 1983.

Filmography
of
Edward Dmytryk

THE HAWK   (Ind)   (1935)
TELEVISION SPY   (Para)   (1939)
EMERGENCY SQUAD   (Para)   (1939)
GOLDEN GLOVES   (Para)   (1939)
MYSTERY SEA RAIDER   (Para)   (1940)
HER FIRST ROMANCE   (I.E. Chadwick)   (1940)
THE DEVIL COMMANDS   (Col)   (1940)
UNDER AGE   (Col)   (1940)
SWEETHEART OF THE CAMPUS   (Col)   (1941)
THE BLONDE FROM SINGAPORE   (Col)   (1941)
SECRETS OF THE LONE WOLF   (Col)   (1941)
CONFESSIONS OF BOSTON BLACKIE   (Col)   (1941)
COUNTER-ESPIONAGE   (Col)   (1942)
SEVEN MILES FROM ALCATRAZ   (RKO)   (1942)
HITLER'S CHILDREN   (RKO)   (1943)
THE FALCON STRIKES BACK   (RKO)   (1943)
CAPTIVE WILD WOMAN   (Univ)   (1943)
BEHIND THE RISING SUN   (RKO)   (1943)
TENDER COMRADE   (RKO)   (1943)
MURDER, MY SWEET   (RKO)   (1944)

BACK TO BATAAN   (RKO)   (1945)
CORNERED   (RKO)   (1945)
TILL THE END OF TIME   (RKO)   (1945)
SO WELL REMEMBERED   (RKO–RANK)   (1946)
CROSSFIRE   (RKO)   (1947)
THE HIDDEN ROOM   (English Ind.)   (1948)
GIVE US THIS DAY   (Eagle-Lion)   (1949)
MUTINY   (King Bros.–U.A.)   (1951)
THE SNIPER   (Kramer–Col)   (1951)
EIGHT IRON MEN   (Kramer–Col)   (1952)
THE JUGGLER   (Kramer–Col)   (1952)
THE CAINE MUTINY   (Kramer–Col)   (1953)
BROKEN LANCE   (20th-Fox)   (1954)
THE END OF THE AFFAIR   (Col)   (1954)
SOLDIER OF FORTUNE   (20th-Fox)   (1955)
THE LEFT HAND OF GOD   (20th-Fox)   (1955)
THE MOUNTAIN   (Para)   (1956)
RAINTREE COUNTY   (MGM)   (1956)
THE YOUNG LIONS   (20th-Fox)   (1957)
WARLOCK   (20th-Fox)   (1958)
THE BLUE ANGEL   (20th-Fox)   (1959)
WALK ON THE WILD SIDE   (Col)   (1961)
THE RELUCTANT SAINT   (Col)   (1961)
THE CARPETBAGGERS   (Para)   (1963)
WHERE LOVE HAS GONE   (Para)   (1964)
MIRAGE   (Univ)   (1965)
ALVAREZ KELLY (Col)   (1966)
ANZIO   (Col)   (1967)
SHALAKO   (Cinerama)   (1968)
BLUEBEARD (Cinerama)   (1972)
THE HUMAN FACTOR   (Bryanston)   (1975)